UNDERSTANDING ASPECTS
The Inconjunct

"An inconjunct is a common aspect, but few people know how they are to be interpreted. We recommend the book highly. It is seminal. It will effect astrological interpretation for many years to come. It solves problems which have blocked us for decades. It is nothing short of brilliant."
— LLEWELLYN NEW TIMES

"In part one of his book Alan Epstein addresses the nature of the issues symbolized by individual planets when involved in inconjuncts. This section, at least as applied to quincunxes, is extremely perceptive and well presented, right down to the summaries at the end of each discussion. In my opinion, this is essential reading for anyone who wants a better understanding of planets in quincunx."
— FRATERNITY FOR CANADIAN ASTROLOGERS, FRATERNITY NEWS

"This book will assist all levels of student and professionals in bridging the gap in the interpretation of aspects, particularly the inconjunct, which is often the most difficult step in chart interpretation on a broader scale."
— NATIONAL COUNCIL FOR GEOCOSMIC RESEARCH NEWSLETTER

UNDERSTANDING ASPECTS

The Inconjunct

ALAN EPSTEIN

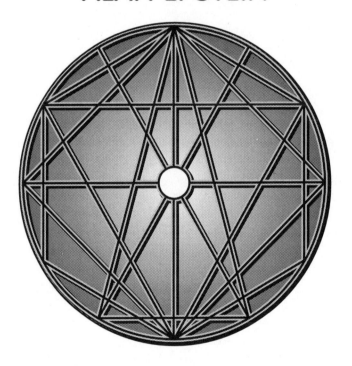

TRINES PUBLISHING

P.O. Box 20548
Reno, Nevada 89515-0548
U S A

UNDERSTANDING ASPECTS
The Inconjunct
by Alan Epstein

TRINES PUBLISHING

P.O. Box 20548
Reno, Nevada 89515-0548
U S A

First Published in 1984 by Samuel Weiser, Inc.
under the title *Psychodynamics of Inconjunctions*

Copyright © 1996, Alan Epstein

Library of Congress Card Number: 95-90905

ISBN: 0-9649783-0-X

10   9   8   7   6   5   4   3   2

Published in association with Conscious Books
Reno, Nevada 1/800-322-9943.

Design and prepress by White Sage Studios
Drawer G, Virginia City, Nevada 89440

Printed and Bound in The United States of America

Table of Contents

Part III – Jimmy Carter's Chart

About the Author
181

Acknowledgements

This book, originally titled *Psychodynamics of Inconjunctions*, was first published in 1984 with the help and encouragement of Betty Lundsted. The evolution of the book began in 1978 as a result of a lecture I did for the New York Chapter of the National Council for Geocosmic Research. Since that time I have received a lot of positive feedback from fellow astrologers who have urged me to get the book back into print.

I want to take this opportunity to thank Greg Nielsen for his help in republishing this book. I also want to thank my friends in the astrology community who encouraged me in this endeavor.

Preface

Understanding Aspects:–The Inconjunct was first published in 1984 by Samuel Weiser, Inc. under the title Psychodynamics of Inconjunctions. I originally became interested in this aspect because of the many quincunxes in my own chart. There wasn't much written about it, at the time, and most astrologers considered it to be a minor aspect. Most of the written material considered the quincunx to to be either a sixth house or eighth house aspect. In any event, it was not thought to be very important.

The original incarnation of this book reflected years of thinking, experimenting, library work, and discussing the aspect with clients. At first I thought only the quincunx to be an inconjunct, but the late Charles Emerson alerted me to the idea that semisextiles might be considered inconjuncts. After much testing, and much resistance, I became convinced that they were. At the time, I couldn't understand why semisextiles were acting exactly like quincunxes, but they surely were.

In the years since the book was published, I've had the opportunity to speak to many astrologers who have confirmed this assessment. I've thought a lot about why the semisextile is an inconjunct, just like the quincunx. It turns out that planets in both semisextile and in quincunx relationship have nothing in common (neither triplicity, quadraplicity or gender). They might, for this reason, be considered as "non aspected" or inconjunct. I urge the reader to verify for himself, whether semisextiles act like quincunxes. The use of the semisextile in chart delineation along with the quincunx will contribute to a richer understanding of the underlying dynamics of the natal chart.

Alan Epstein

PART ONE
Psychodynamics of the Inconjunct

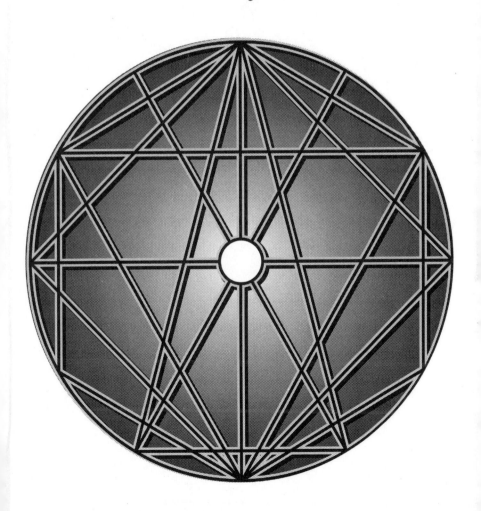

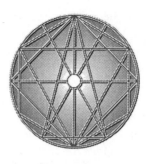

Psychodynamics
of the Inconjunct

Basic Issues

HERE ARE TWO TYPES OF INCONJUNCTS—the quincunx (150°) and the semisextile (30°). Both aspects appear to function in a similar manner and will, therefore, be treated as the same. The term inconjunct will be used to indicate both the semisextile and quincunx.

The basic approach has been to deal with the issues created by the particular aspect. This allows the relationship between seemingly contradictory behavior to be clarified. It permits us to see why people sometimes act completely differently in similar circumstances, with different people.

When something becomes an issue, it becomes a focus of attention, or a problem area. This usually means that, in some way, the factor is out of balance, either through excessiveness or inhibition. This lack of balance may be so noteworthy that a person can be characterized by the excess or lack of the function, or quality. The function, or quality, is an important concern, an issue.

The reader may have observed that when a repressed function is liberated, a person may become temporarily excessive. This occurs until, through excess, he ends his feeling of deprivation by making up for what he feels he has missed. After a while, he feels more comfortable, drops the issue and becomes more moderate. At this stage, the function, or quality, is no longer an issue.

The inconjunct requires the balancing of the desired   against the practicable, the ideal against the real. It requires finding a balance between wish fulfillment and responsibility. The symbols themselves ($\nwarrow\searrow$) give the appearance of a balance or of something being balanced. Using the balance analogy, we can say that on one side is the thing that is desired or required, while on the other side is the price that must be paid in order to attain it. The aspect is more subjective than an opposition, but more objective than a conjunction. It is, therefore, often difficult to define what, exactly, is wanted and why it cannot be attained.

The inconjunct usually manifests as an attitude toward oneself and the world, which insidiously invites self-limitation. The aspect often appears as a need to weigh options. These are usually what to give up or surrender. "You can't have your cake and eat it too," the saying goes, but it seems that this often is exactly what the aspect wants.

One has to give up something to get something else, but the price to be paid (what has to be given up) is unacceptably high. As a result, when the thing is finally attained, the satisfaction is considerably lessened. This causes the person to vacillate and become frustrated. This implies an immature attachment to the object of desire, or a paralysis of will. Also implied is an attitude of ego imbalance and a necessity to grow up. The major challenge is to grow from immature desire toward maturity, flexibility and realistic appraisal of life circumstances.

One of the basic meanings of the inconjunct is adjustment. From this, many other meanings may be derived. Adjustment implies that accustomed ways of functioning are inadequate to present conditions. Either external circumstances or internal psychodynamics create a problem for the person. Old ways of functioning no longer seem adequate to meet current challenges. Conditions require him to find new solutions.

In the process, he must recognize and accept the demands of manifesting reality. He may have to review his accustomed attitudes and come to terms with his defects. This is, of course, a most difficult thing to do. Humans tend to settle in a groove and become complacent. There is a strong tendency to function automatically. The pressure to adjust is seen as an irritant. There is a tendency to think, "Why can't things go along as they always have? Why can't I have things the way I want them?" The answer is simple: If the person was meant to be a vegetable, he would have incarnated as one and not as a human being.

Another basic meaning of the inconjunct involves trade-offs. Trade-offs require analysis and weighing of the need or want against the cost of attaining it. The person usually wants more than one thing and is confronted with the need to choose between equally desirable or undesirable alternatives. He winds up with a percentage of each rather than the whole, and the disappointment ruins the satisfaction. This is, therefore, an aspect of partial success; of having to settle for the attainable; of having to moderate ideals; of settling for less than perfection.

This aspect will often describe problems at work or on projects the individual is involved with. Practical limitations such as time or money may become restrictions which must be dealt with. In personal relationships, unconscious fears or needs for acceptance may induce the person to deny himself in order to preserve the relationship. These are trade-offs which spring from the need to be liked by everyone.

A third type of trade-off is the one that involves internal self-images. The individual becomes accustomed to thinking of himself in a certain way, and this self-conception limits growth and development. He cannot see himself doing something and either will refuse to try or program himself for failure in order to satisfy his internal self-image. He wants to succeed and be happy, but he knows who he is – he must not be happy or succeed, because this will require him to alter the old self-conception.

Closely related to trade-offs is the issue of compromise. Compromise means flexibility and the need to retain an open mind. Rigid attitudes often create an impasse, and it is only the ability to step away from rigid positions that permits frozen issues to be resolved. However, to some people, life is a series of compromises. They never seem to assert their needs. They seem compelled, either by external events or their own fears, to compromise on even minor issues. As a consequence, they often are frustrated, sometimes to the point of bitterness.

These people need to learn the art of compromise, which includes knowing when not to compromise. They must learn that it is all right to say no, and to take the risks saying no may involve. They need to learn that others ultimately don't respect too much compliancy.

The inconjunct can also result in the opposite attitude toward compromise. Some people stubbornly refuse to concede, even on relatively minor matters. They may refuse to listen. When they do listen, they have already set up such barriers to exchange of views that they are certain to reject other ways of seeing or doing things. These people may be reacting against the past, against a time when they were forced to submit in contradiction to strong feelings of disagreement. Now that they are free and on their own, they will allow no one to force them to compromise again. Sometimes, this refusal to concede becomes a defense against closeness with others. They may actually feel weak and view compromise as a confirmation of their inner weakness.

In both these cases, the issue of compromise assumes neurotic proportions.

There is, however, a healthy attitude toward compromise. It merely means review and reassessment for the purpose of finding a solution to a problem. This requires a determination of the validity of one's attitudes or actions, and a willingness to make adjustments where necessary.

The inconjunct can, as an aspect of compromise, cause a review of attitudes and actions taken for granted. People who use the aspect well have the capability of inducing or challenging others to reassess their beliefs and entertain different possibilities. This can be a most potent aspect for those who are involved in teaching or social change. They can induce others to adjust their views, which, in turn, ultimately affects the way society functions.

The art of compromise requires an ability to review, reconsider, re-evaluate, and modify. The inconjunct, by confronting us with the necessity of compromise, forces us to develop these latent abilities. It is a reality aspect, forcing us to deal with our desires as they contradict the requirements of the external world. It demands that we be practical and learn how to make things work. When things no longer work, it forces us to re-examine our accustomed precepts and practices. It guarantees frustration as long as desire is pitted against the requirements of manifest reality. With the surrender of neurotic wants and acceptance of the world as it is, rather than what it ought to be, frustration is relieved.

Mastery of the art of compromise leads to development of an ability to negotiate, which is another ramification of the inconjunct. One learns to recognize what is possible and what will work; as well as to recognize what is not possible and what will frustrate. One learns to anticipate potential impasse situations, and how to avoid them. One learns how to cooperate, how much to assert, and when to retreat from a position. This is the game of human interaction played on a very high level. The ultimate end is development of the ability to assist people to come to terms with each other, and to facilitate cooperative efforts between potential adversaries.

The inconjunct can be a neurotic aspect involving dissatisfaction, complaining, frustration or ill health. It often shows where the individual refuses to face reality. It can create a situation of extreme stubbornness or extreme compliance. Under these conditions, the individual's life is one of utter frustration.

Acceptance becomes an overwhelming issue and the individual will do just about anything to prove himself or ingratiate himself with others. Real relationship flies out the window as he tries to gain respect, acceptance and approval in self-destructive ways.

He ultimately grows to resent the unfairness of his lot in life. He secretly compares himself with others, and feels bitter over the sacrifices he must make, just to be loved and accepted. But, no matter how great the sacrifices, it seems he cannot make people accept or love him. He feels unlovable, and apologetic for his existence, so he tries to earn tolerance from others. When he gets stuck on this carousel, there is no easy way off. Attempts to purchase love do not work, because he feels prostituted and does not respect himself. If he does not respect himself, how can others respect him? And, even if they did, would he be willing to accept their respect?

This would require a compromise in the basic self-image of unworthiness. Until he is willing to re-evaluate himself and modify the inner image, he remains stuck in old ways of relating. The inner belief system, which says that he is not worthy of respect or love, prevents external satisfaction as long as it is operable. Thus, the first and most profound compromise is in regard to inner self-images. Will he face reality and accept the fact that the past is merely an image in his mind, or will he steadfastly cling to that inner picture? The picture of inner unworthiness is what drives him to living self-destructively. When he can revise that picture, the neurotic behavior which brings unhappiness will cease.

SYNTHESIS

This book has been divided into two parts. Part I addresses the psycho-dynamic issues surrounding each planetary inconjunct. For example, the section about the Sun is generally true for all inconjuncts involving the Sun. However, to understand the specific psychodynamic issues, we must look to the planet on the other end of the aspect and integrate its meaning with the first. With a Sun-Mars inconjunct, it would be best to read the sections in Part I for both the Sun and Mars and integrate them. This synthesis may reveal that solar inconjunct behavior is concerned with or motivated by Mars inconjunct concerns. The reverse may also be true.

After reading the sections on the Sun and Mars, turn to Part II, and read Sun Inconjunct Mars, in order to ascertain which of these possible manifestations is actually the case. Noting this, it might be wise to return to both Sun and Mars sections in Part I in order to assess the underlying psychodynamic issues. This can provide a key to personality and character which will have to be integrated within the chart as a whole.

Needless to say, the inconjunct is merely one factor which must be considered with and weighed against other indications in the chart – the sign and house placement and the other aspect configurations.

ORBS

The essential meaning of this aspect is related to the interaction between planets in completely dissimilar signs. Thus, planets inconjunct by sign carry a greater orb than those inconjunct by degree. For example, planets in inconjunct aspect in the signs Pisces and Libra will carry a greater orb than planets in inconjunct aspect in, say, early Pisces and late Virgo.

The reader might want to start by using an 8 degree orb for planets inconjunct by sign, and then expand the orb allowance as he gains experience with this aspect. I would recommend limiting the orb allowance for out of sign inconjuncts to only one or two degrees.

KEYWORDS

adjustment
trade-offs
compromise
reconsideration
re-evaluation
modification
review
negotiation
dissatisfaction
frustration
sacrifice
defiance
inability to give and take
lack of moderation
abstinence vs. indulgence
inability to say no
needing to prove oneself
seeking something from people who won't give it

SUN

The Sun is the source of life, the center of the solar system, and, thus, by analogy, the center of consciousness. It is the inner light and creative spirit, which bestows the gift of life. It indicates the essential spirit, central purpose and inner meaning of life. The Sun, therefore, rules the inner direction, intention, and purpose of individual lives. The healthy solar function encourages us to confidence and creative activity, but the disturbed solar function draws us into peripheral concerns, self-alienation and struggle for existence.

The solar inconjunct indicates a tendency to feel unwanted or unneeded. One, therefore, unconsciously begs others to tolerate or accept one's existence. This generally stems from a childhood experience of being unwanted, unneeded, a nuisance or a chore to the parents. The parents may have wanted a child of the opposite sex. The father may have been absent or rejecting. He may have worked long hours or avoided his family because of his relationship with the mother. In any event, this will be interpreted as father rejection by the individual with this aspect. The native may have blamed himself for his father's avoidance of the family. Consequently, he develops a defensive attitude about his existence. He must prove that his existence is beneficial to others, beginning with his parents. Self-justification becomes a big issue. He learns to justify himself to himself, and to others, so that he can feel worthy of existing, and so that others will tolerate him. He learns to earn the right to be accepted.

He induces people to accept his company by fulfilling some purpose. The other end of the aspect indicates the purpose he adopts. The consequence of adopting a purpose in order to justify one's existence is the abandonment and loss of one's original life purpose. Thus, another theme of the solar inconjunct is the continual seeking of direction. This person senses that he is being untrue to himself, and that his life lacks meaning, because he has adopted an alien purpose, just to earn the right to be tolerated. The search for meaning and purpose assumes great importance.

However, some natives may adopt a lifestyle that is blatantly objectionable to others, and defiantly live it. They assert their right to exist on their own terms and refuse to admit that they may be wrong.

This person soon learns to play a role and project an image. (The role is one in which he earlier found acceptance.) It becomes his primary way of relating. The role becomes so ingrained that he totally identifies with it, like the actor who becomes the part he is playing. The role becomes the person, and the real person hides behind the role. Of course, when one lives a role, one lives a fiction. Somewhere in his psyche, self-doubt begins to develop. While he plays the role, he is defended and invulnerable. No one sees the real person. If he should be rejected, it is the role, not himself, that is rejected.

Situations or relationships are sought in which to perform the role. He attracts people who prey on his need for acceptance by withholding it. This person may subtly manipulate situations to set the stage for his role, so that he can relate in accordance with it.

Sooner or later, he comes to feel dissatisfied with his life and begins to search for meaning. He then has to confront his act, his facade, and consider dropping it, in order to begin living his real life. He begins to confront the inner fears and sorrows, the games he plays, and his resentment at having to play them. He then has to deal with the shock of discovering his life as a hypocritical ploy to gain acceptance.

The task of dropping the act is extremely difficult, because he has so totally become the act that he does not know how to live outside it. He confronts his attitude, manner, life style, clothing, body posture, etc. How can he drop the act when he seems to fall into it so easily?

Obviously, awareness is the key. He needs to become aware of what he is doing, from moment to moment. He must see how he manipulates others into supporting his act, and then begin to discard it. He needs to learn to relate anew, and this, of course, is very threatening.

The challenge of this aspect is to relate without apology or justification. The solar inconjunct suggests that this person experienced the father either as weak or as rigid and uncompromising. The native may have responded by either adopting an equivalent or opposite life posture. Perhaps the father constantly made excuses or justified himself to others. This aspect also may indicate an avoidance of the father, or a refusal to compromise with him.

The solar inconjunct indicates the potential for developing a dominating nature. The person may attempt to arrange his environment to suit himself, without thought or concern for others. This betrays a self-concern which stems from improper childhood attention. As a child he may have been generally neglected, and then given excessive attention to make up for it. There may have been swings of parental attention from one extreme to another, depending upon how he acted. This might cause him to become uncomfortable, when given attention. He may, therefore, seek to avoid attention-getting situations.

In some cases, however, the need for attention might be so great that this person might learn how to divert attention to himself. He becomes a performer; he learns the role which will get him attention and plays it again and again. He may feel lost outside the role. This can have disastrous consequences when the role loses its appropriateness. This predicament is typical of those who are given excessive attention during childhood, because of their precocity. Most of them cannot carry this precocity into adulthood and, thus, lose the feeling of being special They tend to retreat into private memories and dwell upon past accomplishments.

This aspect indicates difficulty in finding direction. The individual may wander aimlessly, unsure of his purposes or how to actualize them. It may also manifest as a lack of determination. Lack of self-acceptance puts his intentions in doubt. Circumstances can force him to compromise his purposes, and revise his decisions.

He may be so preoccupied with acceptance that he becomes over-concerned with validity. This may lead him to become proof oriented. He must be able to prove his validity, so that others will have no grounds for rejecting him. He ultimately must come to realize that people may accept or reject him based solely upon their preinclinations, regardless of the validity of his ideas or purposes. He must accept the world as biased, and continue to pursue his interests, without concern about rejection. This, of course, means acceptance of others, including their faults. This allows him to accept his own efforts, even though they are imperfect, and follow through on his decisions.

This inconjunct sometimes indicates disturbances centering around ambition. The person may be extremely ambitious, or completely lacking in ambition. In the first case, his goals are directed toward becoming important. He will rise to the top and force others to accept him. He may have an *I'll-show-them!* attitude. He may force his way into situations where he is unwanted or unaccepted. He may be attracted to interests which others reject, and doing so, he re-experiences his early life rejection. He makes it his purpose to force others to accept his interests. He must, again, prove his worth and validity by justifying his projects.

Sometimes, ambition may be an attempt to prove himself to his father. He tries to convince his father to accept him by attaining honors. This aspect sometimes indicates that the person may be imitating the father, who was a high achiever or important person.

In the case where the person seems to be lacking in ambition, this may indicate a reluctance to compete with the father. Lack of ambition may be a severe reaction against an ambitious or successful father.

The solar inconjunct may indicate an imbalance in body/mind. One may reject the body instead of honoring its requirements. In other cases, the person may become very body – health conscious.

In this respect, the aspect can be an indicator of health issues in one's life. The aspect may motivate the person to become a health or exercise enthusiast. It may reveal a potential health weakness. The aspect may sometimes indicate health problems in childhood, which led the person to feel inferior. The feeling may linger, as a motivating factor, even though the health condition no longer exists.

In some cases, the aspect may indicate that the father suffered a serious health problem, which interfered with his ability to relate to the native. In this case, the aspect can indicate the concessions that had to be made to the father because of his poor health.

Another manifestation of this aspect is a concern with finding meaningful work. Work, for this person, becomes the essential element in finding meaning in life. The closer the orb of the aspect, the more crucial the concern. He cannot settle for the schizoid life style most of us are forced to live. Most of us do unfulfilling work in order to get the money to pay the rent, and put food on the table. We find our fulfillment in our avocations rather than in our vocations. This is why we require vacations. The solar inconjunct person is different. He feels his life to be essentially meaningless unless he can find purpose in his work. When he finds his work, he finds meaning and direction. He has taken a gigantic step toward finding satisfaction in life. His vocation may eventually form the core of his life philosophy.

The solar inconjunct may move the person to assume the role of negotiator or compromiser. He may also be a critic. He takes it upon himself to express dissatisfaction in whatever field he is interested. He, therefore, plays the role of criticizer, and if he is not careful, he may become Mr. Critic.

Basically, he is a searcher for truth and meaning, purpose and validity. He may confront others and get them to reconsider their decisions. His task is to create a cooperative effort between unrelating principles and so learn to master the real world. He performs his service to us all, helps and heals while he works at perfecting the art of living.

This is an aspect of potential leadership. It gives the dedication and a sense of inner direction that can inspire others to purposeful activity. These natives, therefore, make good executives. The aspect may also be useful for theater pursuits, such as acting or playwriting. These people may also make good guidance counselors and therapists, because they can help people find meaning in work and life. They may become natural philosophers or teachers who convey to others the fruits of their search for meaning in life.

Summary

Hiding behind a role in life. The role becomes the basis of relationship with others. There is an attempt to project an image to others.

Feeling unwanted or unneeded. There is an attraction to situations where one is unwanted; a tendency to create circumstances which make others reject one; an attraction to associations or situations from which one is or will be excluded.

Feeling compelled to apologize. These natives adopt an apologetic manner. Some may refuse to apologize, even when they are wrong. They may develop an extreme attitude toward apology, either demanding it as a matter of principle or refusing to accept any form of apology.

Self-justification. The native continually justifies himself to himself, and to others. He may also require others to justify themselves to him.

Lack of direction or purpose. The native vacillates in his intentions or may be rigid and uncompromising. He is uncertain of his self-identity, and constantly seeks meaning in life. This aspect is ultimately related to the problem of finding meaningful work.

MOON

The Moon rules subjective perception. It is the emotional factor, the invisible link between ourselves and others, which attunes us to the social context of existence and, therefore, has a great deal to do with self-image and social conditioning. It defines our day-to-day feelings, and our ability to interact socially. The Moon has a tremendous impact upon the quality of our lives. The healthy lunar function informs us of the inner reactions of others, and permits us to respond in an organic way. Disturbances in this function tend to alienate us from others and reduce the quality of our lives.

The lunar inconjunct indicates problems in emotional expressiveness, either nonexpressiveness or overemotionality. The feeling and expressive functions have been disturbed and this results in emotive problems.

The problems usually stem from a necessity to repress feelings in child-hood. The parents of this native may have been emotionally inexpressive or repressed, depriving the native or emotional warmth and contact.

Every child requires emotional contact from its parents, especially from its mother. Every child needs approval and encouragement. When mother is emotionally absent, the child may interpret this as disapproval. Mother may actually express disapproval or withhold approval unless certain conditions are met. The child becomes concerned with winning approval and avoiding disapproval.

Approval/disapproval, therefore, becomes the foremost consideration, and one's efforts become oriented toward winning approval, or avoiding or defying disapproval. One may then only participate in approved activities or, defiantly, in disapproved ones. One may attempt to excel just for the approval it will bring.

This person may develop a block to winning approval and revert to acceptance of disapproval. He may then participate in what are generally considered disapproved of activities, and may not know how to accept approval when it is given.

The other side of this behavior is the development of a disapproving attitude. This person may become critical and force people to win his approval. Such an attitude creates a barrier to relationship because he constantly sits in judgement of others.

There is a tendency to develop a strong internal judge who takes the fun and spontaneity out of life. The individual gets caught up in judging himself and others, because he has learned only one way of relating – approval/disapproval. He constantly seeks approval, and at the same time, sees others in a disapproving light. It is ironic but, because he so desperately wants others to approve of him, he disapproves of them.

One of the manifestations of this aspect is the experience of shame and humiliation. This person may have been humiliated by one of the parents, especially the mother. The stinging memory of the humiliations may cause avoidance of or attraction to potentially embarrassing situations. Habitual childhood humiliations create a conditioned response which anticipates further humiliations. This person may learn avoidance behavior, and become socially inhibited. He may act out the opposite extreme and seek revenge against the parent through current relationships. There are times the native may be ashamed and disapproving of the parents' physical appearance, intelligence or lack of knowledge. He may act out of this motif by becoming involved with people who humiliate him or whom he shames and humiliates.

Lunar inconjunct people are extremely sensitive to betrayal. There is a tendency to see unexpected disappointments as possible betrayal. They may be drawn to people who will betray them. When this happens, they re-experience the deep disappointment and humiliation of childhood. They become suspicious and demand loyalty from others. They stand ready to accuse others of betrayal – in fact, they expect it! Once the feared happens, no explanations are acceptable, and relationships are severed.

This person may also attract people who demand complete loyalty from him. He feels constantly pressured by their readiness to accuse him of betrayal. He may assume that people have this attitude, even when they do not. He may create this concern in friends through indiscretions and minor betrayals. In this way, he seems to surround himself with the issue.

This behavior may re-enact childhood circumstances in which the parents accused him of betrayal or punished him for minor indiscretions. His attraction to people who accuse him of betrayal is basically oriented to convincing them to drop the issue, which, of course, they will not do. If he does betray people, he may be attempting to recreate the childhood issue so that he can convince them to forgive and forget, as he wanted his parents to do. The trouble is that once they forgive and forget, he may recreate the issue again. He remains trapped in this pattern until he becomes acutely aware of it.

Other natives may become obsessed with perfect loyalty. They go to extremes to prove themselves loyal. They are inordinately ethical and stand firmly behind their word.

People with lunar inconjuncts tend to vacillate emotionally. This indicates short lived emotions, the emotional chameleon, or the person susceptible to the emotional appeals of others. The other manifestation is emotional fixation. This individual becomes fixed in regard to feeling, and cannot change emotional attitudes when necessary.

Both extremes indicate difficulty in emotional re-evaluation stemming from having to adjust to inconsistent or fickle parents. If the parents of this individual punished him for not having feelings they approved of, he may have had to feign the proper feelings in order to avoid punishment. If his parents were emotionally fickle, he may have developed a similar pattern through imitation. Some natives, however, may react against these pressures by resolving to stand firmly behind their feelings. This describes another motivation for the fixed emotional attitudes described earlier.

The lunar inconjunct may indicate that the parents were emotionally rigid. This rigidity may have been so extreme that they could only express one emotion, such as constant sadness or fear or anger. Consequently, this native may be oversensitized to that particular emotion. He may be fixed in the emotion or will react against it so strongly that he tends to avoid it. He may attract emotionally rigid people who overemphasize the emotion to which he is so sensitized. This oversensitivity may lead to severe overreactions, such as extreme resentment or flight, which make others feel inhibited in expressing the emotion. As a consequence, the emotion comes to form a barrier between the native and others.

This aspect also indicates a possible need to hide feelings from others, especially painful feelings. This may stem from a childhood decision to avoid revealing just how hurt he was. He is attempting to retain self-respect by avoiding humiliation, laughter or derision at his open show of emotion. He may have come to deny the expression of a particular emotion or, possibly, all emotion. The latter case can lead to an emotional blandness which will be difficult to overcome.

There are self-image problems with this aspect. The person may vacillate in his self-perception, which re-enacts parental tendencies to vacillate in their attitudes toward themselves and him. He may have developed contrary self-images which contend with each other for supremacy. He may suffer from a self-image of weakness and indecision. He may fear others' perceptions of him as weak and vacillating, and attempt to compensate by being firmer. He may become so firm that he has difficulty accepting people's perceptions of him. This discourages them from offering him any feedback. It also makes him prone to misunderstand how others feel about him, and why they feel that way. He loses the ability to assess his impact upon others, and is unable to understand or anticipate their reactions.

This inconjunct tends to increase emotional impressionability. The native can be quite empathic and compassionate and, in some cases, receptivity can be so strong that the individual is inundated with the feelings picked up from others. This may lead him to fear being overwhelmed by their feelings.

He may, therefore, out of a need to defend himself, completely cut off his feelings or become anti-sympathetic and view compassion as a form of weakness. This behavior stems from the childhood experience of being completely open and vulnerable. He may have felt victimized by feelings which were not his own and eventually come to hate this sensitivity and learned to block empathic feelings. His appearance of coolness and lack of sympathy is a defense against being overwhelmed again.

This aspect may be useful for working with the public and for influencing people through emotional appeal. It might, therefore, find an outlet in advertising. It might be utilized in fields as diverse as art, music, theater or psychology, where the ability to understand and modify feelings is important.

Summary

Emotional restraint. The native finds himself having to inhibit or hide his feelings. He may have difficulty expressing feelings appropriately. These difficulties range from emotional repression to emotional excess.

Approval/disapproval. The native can be judgmental, and he fears others are judging him. He is concerned with winning approval or avoiding disapproval. He also may take a disapproving attitude toward others.

Defiance. This is a compensatory reaction to the expectation of disapproval. The native may purposely do the very things of which others disapprove as an act of defiant self-assertion.

Embarrassment or humiliation. The native may avoid potentially embarrassing situations. He also may be attracted to people who will embarrass or humiliate him, or he may embarrass or humiliate others. He can be very shy.

Betrayal. The native is hypersensitive to betrayal. He demands complete loyalty and tends to see disappointment as betrayal. He may attract people who betray him or who accuse him of betrayal.

MERCURY

Mercury rules objective perception. It is the rational-perceptive factor that links us to the physical world. It rules thought and communication, which permits us to express our needs and intentions to others. It is the medium through which we share experiences and learn from others. It permits us to organize data and develop practical solutions to life's problems. When this function is disrupted, there are difficulties in internal thinking, interpersonal communication and rational interaction with others.

The Mercury inconjunct indicates a disturbance in the ability to communicate. There seems to be a lack of confidence in one's rational faculties, intelligence or perceptions. There may be a need to prove or defend one's intelligence. If this need is overwhelming, the person with this aspect may become intellectually timid.

There may have been embarrassment over his intelligence during childhood. Perhaps he was a slow learner and was insulted by parents or peers who treated him as if he were stupid. Perhaps there was embarrassment because he was too intelligent. He may have felt that he was labeled as different and, therefore, pushed away.

The Mercury inconjunct indicates that the native's parents generally avoided communicating with him when he was young (even if he was considered bright), and treated his remarks or questions with indifference or impatience. In the case of the bright student, this will result in a clear double message: that he is intelligent, but not really. This dichotomy will effectively undermine his feelings of intelligence. In the case of the slow learner, it will reinforce his feelings of intellectual inferiority. As a result, he may avoid mental effort (because he fears or avoids the challenge), or he may feel compelled to prove or defend his intelligence.

If his parents contradicted him, he may contradict people or be intolerant of contradiction. He may issue disclaimers, or be extremely sensitive about the acceptance of his ideas. He creates obstacles to free discussion because he tends to take honest questioning as an attack upon his views. Communication depends upon free exchange. This person can discourage discussion by asserting his views with such vehemence that a free exchange of ideas is impossible. There is often a take-it-or-leave-it attitude which leaves no room for sharing or modification of ideas.

Sometimes, however, the exact opposite occurs. The individual may become reluctant to share his views because he anticipates contradiction and criticism. In this frame of mind, he sees any criticism as a personal attack. This results in the stifling of discussion. Other people may have additional information but are reluctant to share it because of his obdurate attitude. Their views are kept to themselves and, so, an opportunity to learn is lost. When information is proffered, it is likely to be greeted harshly, or rejected if it varies with what he has already decided.

People with this aspect seem to be attracted to unpopular ideas. This tends to recreate the childhood situation. In the process, they challenge views which have been accepted or taken for granted. People responding to this challenge are forced to reassess the ideas called into question. This, in effect, instigates a search for the truth on a conceptual level.

These natives tend to be attracted to intellectually rigid people who reject or even ridicule their ideas or intelligence. They become caught in an old pattern of intellectual rejection, and waste time and energy trying to convince rejecting people of their worth.

The Mercury inconjunct often manifests as withholding knowledge or information. The person with this aspect fears that what he reveals may be used against him. When he was a child, his parents may have induced him to speak and then punished him for what he said. This will create a need to keep silent or hold his tongue. Perhaps he was criticized or punished whenever he spoke up. Perhaps he was forced to speak softly or be unnaturally quiet.

He may also have been forced to adopt patterns of indirect communication. This might, in extreme circumstances, lead to lying or dissembling. He may have learned to be crafty and tell his parents what they wanted to hear because it was too dangerous to speak truthfully. If his parents were untruthful with him, he will have learned to question what he is being told. He may have developed an expectation of being lied to.

If things were exaggerated, minimized, or merely alluded to, he may have learned to exaggerate, minimize, or allude to things himself. In some cases, parental actions contradicted their words. This can lead him to become a stickler for keeping one's word.

This aspect can also indicate problems in perception. During childhood, the individual may have had to deny what he saw because it was too threatening, and may have even grown to question the validity of his perceptions, perhaps even dulled the sharpness of his senses. He might now either challenge others with his perceptions, or be so dependent upon their perceptions that he tends to see things through their eyes.

On another level, this aspect can indicate empathic abilities. This person needs to be aware, however, of the danger of losing himself in other people's perceptions.

Additional issues indicated by this aspect include problems with sibling or peer rivalry. This individual may have felt compromised by his siblings. Perhaps his parents talked to his brothers and sisters but ignored him. Perhaps secrets were kept from him. If he was punished because siblings betrayed him to his parents, he will have learned to be cautious or crafty. He may develop a belief that he can't trust people with his private thoughts. This can result in a secretive personality who feels utterly compromised when others learn his private thoughts.

If his siblings slandered him to his parents, he may be sensitized to the prospect of being misquoted or misunderstood. He may attract people who are prone to gossip or talk about him behind his back. He may find himself misrepresented or misunderstood, again and again, in some sort of parallel to his early life experience. On the other hand, the opposite is always possible. This individual may gossip and misquote others.

There is a great sensitivity to plagiarism. He will have unusually strong feelings about it and refuse to participate in anything even suggestive of it. This may be a strong reaction to the experience of being plagiarized early in life. Conversely, he may move in the opposite direction and plagiarize others. He feels the urge to communicate but lacks confidence in his own intellectual capacities.

Sometimes, this aspect indicates parental punishment of the native by means of the "silent treatment." The parent may resort to silence over an extended period, which, in effect, reduces the native to a nonperson. As a result, he may grow up fearing exclusion and rejection. He may recreate the ostracism experience through rebellious speech, or he may so fear ostracism that he meekly goes along with others in order to avoid the possibility of offending them.

A typical manifestation of this aspect is exceedingly blunt, direct or defiant speech. This type tends to speak or state opinions in a challenging way, to cut off debate or reply through the manner of presentation. Sometimes, the native will become self-deprecating. He may speak in a disarming manner, perhaps using humor, playacting, clowning or miming. This aspect, therefore, can describe a mime or entertainer. It might be used effectively in communication through nonverbal means. It can be used by someone who wishes to communicate through allusion or metaphor.

The Mercury inconjunct gives the potential for balancing various viewpoints and incorporating new data or information into prevailing views. It creates an ability to take a number of things into account, and can lead to an open-mindedness and liberality of thought. It forces one to open one's mind and accept contrary viewpoints.

This can be a most effective aspect for a writer or communicator of new ideas, because it offers the possibility of causing others to reconsider their views. It can be used by a writer or journalist who is concerned with getting people to change their views. The concern with new ideas and veracity of beliefs can lead one to challenge old, dogmatic viewpoints.

The aspect teaches us to present new information or criticism in an acceptable way so that others will listen. Humor, allegory and metaphor allow us to present potentially threatening information less directly, or in a disarming manner. Confrontation often causes defensiveness, whereas communication through allegory or humor allows others to participate in a new way. It is as if they have deciphered and discovered it for themselves. Since it is their realization, they are more willing to accept it.

Summary

Flow of information. The native tends to hide his thoughts and withhold information. He may purposely dissemble or attract people who withhold information from him. He may hide his intelligence. He may tell people what they want to hear, and allude to things rather than speak directly.

Self-expression creates problems. The native tends to say things that displease others. He gets into trouble because of his views or because of the way he says things. He is attracted to ideas which others will resist. He feels misunderstood. Others misrepresent him and distort his meaning.

Difficulty in communication. The native may find it hard to communicate effectively. He may feel lacking in knowledge or fear that others will ridicule him when he speaks. He may be reluctant to speak up or ask questions because he fears others will consider the question or remark stupid. It may become important for him to prove his intelligence.

Difficulty in accepting criticism. The native tends to take criticism of his ideas as a personal attack. This makes it difficult to discuss things objectively with him. He tends either to gossip or be the victim of gossip. He fears or anticipates slander. He may become the victim of slander.

Manner of speech. The native may speak in an extremely blunt or defiant manner, which precludes opposition to his ideas. He may sometimes use a humorous or self-deprecating approach. This, too, is an attempt to allay opposition.

VENUS

Venus is the principle of relaxation. It rules satisfaction and pleasure. Pleasure leads to relaxation and relaxation permits enjoyment. Venus is part of the basic feedback system which informs us of the degree of security in our environment and the degree of completion of our tasks. It is a socializing factor, which prompts us to reach out in a loving way in order to commune with the divine spark in others, or to bestow upon them the inner light of our spirit. Venus difficulties are, therefore, indicators of discomfort and personal insecurity.

The Venus inconjunct indicates difficulty with self-worth, reflecting a childhood in which parents used love as a reward. The experience of being conditionally loved creates a feeling of intrinsic unlovability and un-worthiness. This causes many social difficulties.

The individual with this inconjunct may have difficulty making social contacts or feel uncomfortable in social situations. He feels a need to win people over, and constantly attempt to ingratiate himself with others. He, therefore, attracts people who prey upon his low self-esteem for their advantage.

He attracts manipulative people, who treat him poorly, and demand favors as a precondition for love. He also attracts people who withhold love or appreciation. He feels put upon, used and unappreciated.

People with this aspect often find it difficult to accept love or appre-ciation gracefully. They tend to reject those who appreciate them and are attracted to those who are indifferent, or who withhold love. They either drive away potential friends or manipulate them into withholding affection.

This is the classic case of the person who cannot take a compliment. He works hard for appreciation but feels uncomfortable when he gets it. This happens because the mind is more preoccupied with resolving painful memories than with accepting new satisfactions. Relief of pain has the highest priority in the psyche. New pleasures are, therefore, shunted aside as the old problems are recreated over and over, until they are resolved.

The native may have an image of himself as awkward and unattractive; he may be self-conscious or vain. This is because he either was made to feel unattractive as a child, or received excessive attention for his cuteness or beauty. Consequently, an aberration about his personal appearance may have developed. If he grew up feeling inferior, he either takes extra-ordinary measures to enhance his appearance or gives up and neglects to groom himself.

Appearance is an important issue because people commonly form judgments based upon first impressions. Those natives who opt for intensive grooming often go overboard to perfect their appearance. They can become fastidious, self-centered or critical. They may take great pains to perfect themselves, fretting over minor imperfections even though they appear attractive to others. They believe that their popularity depends upon physical attractiveness. There may be a fear of reverting back to their basic unattractive state. This concern may be reinforced by surrounding themselves with, or comparing themselves to, exceptionally attractive people. This concern with beauty may ultimately cause these individuals to become more concerned with surface appearance than inner content.

The other reaction to feelings of unattractiveness is to steadfastly maintain the old image. These people may, therefore, refuse to take even minor steps to enhance their appearance. They want affection even though they are plain or unattractive. They keep themselves unattractive and then pity themselves for being unloved. And, if they should find someone to love them, they flee from or push the other person away. These people are really more interested in re-enacting the past as a frozen ritual than accepting new possibilities.

The Venus inconjunct often indicates difficulties with gratification. This individual may have a low tolerance for certain pleasures or may be overindulgent in others. He may forego pleasure while still desiring it. The problem sometimes manifests as a battle of will against desire. This may be part of a spiritual discipline practiced by the person.

The issue tends to arise from pleasure deprivation in childhood, based in negative parental attitudes toward love and sexuality. During childhood, the native may have been punished for indulging in self-gratification, and may have developed anxiety in relation to feeling natural biological pleasures and sensations. If the parents were emotionally blocked or detached and substituted food, toys, etc., for emotional warmth, the native will learn to accept material things as substitutes for emotional warmth. He may, thus, become materialistic instead of loving. He may turn to food as a substitute for love. He ultimately becomes dependent upon things (or people as things).

He becomes a collector of property, possessions, money or people, and feels threatened by the possibility of losing any of this accumulation. He feels uncomfortable with pleasure and finds it difficult to be naturally responsive to life's satisfactions. He either submits to his internal censor or seeks out forbidden fruits. This disrupts the ease and joy of simple interaction. Rather than relating straightforwardly, his pleasure needs are satisfied in all sorts of distorted ways. People are treated more as pleasure objects than kindred spirits.

Typical of this aspect is an inability to demand appropriate rewards. These people find it difficult to engage in the necessary social barter, either withdrawing behind anxiety and self-pity or making exorbitant demands upon others. Negotiating is difficult, both on a material and psychial level.

Thus, we find the person who works for low wages, in the hope that he will be appreciated, or the professional who finds it hard to ask for proper remuneration. In other cases, we find people who demand excessive compensation for their efforts. On a social level, we find the person who is helpful to others, often going out of his way and foregoing his own needs. He wants to win love or appreciation, but does not know how to accept it when it is offered.

These attitudes may stem from parental accusations of ungratefulness. The native may have been taught to accept whatever little was given. Perhaps the parents supervised him too closely and overruled his personal preferences. He may have learned to forego his own needs to please others. This aspect sometimes indicates a tendency to make personal sacrifices in order to attain love. The beloved, for whom the sacrifices are made, is usually oblivious or unappreciative. The native may become bitter and spiteful and turn on his beloved with the full power of fury. He may spitefully sacrifice his own joy in order to deny happiness to the other. This is similar, in some ways, to the Medea story.

This aspect can give talent in art, music or other aesthetic pursuits. The ability to make an attractive presentation may be developed. This can be useful in such diverse fields as packaging, sales, advertising or theater. This aspect might also be utilized in spiritual pursuits such as meditation.

The Venus inconjunct eventually comes to terms with appearance and value as important ingredients in human interaction. The value of money is learned, and self-consciousness is overcome. The giving and accepting of pleasure is learned, and a healthy respect for the material dimension of life is developed.

Summary

Love deprivation. The native wants to be liked by everyone and may try to ingratiate himself with others in order to obtain the affirmation he needs. He tries to win love or appreciation from unresponsive people. He is vulnerable to manipulation through the withholding of love.

Self-worth problems. The native suffers from low self-esteem. He may have difficulty obtaining appropriate compensation for his efforts: He charges either too little or too much. He may become avaricious and measure his worth by the quantity of his possessions.

Low pleasure tolerance. The native finds it difficult to relax and enjoy himself. He may find it hard to attain gratification. On the other hand, an excessive need for gratification may be displayed. He runs from pleasure to pleasure, never fully enjoying himself.

Personal attractiveness. The native may take great pains to perfect his personal appearance, and develop the ability to charm others. He may become superficial. Sometimes, even minor efforts to enhance appearance is resisted. He demands love even though he keeps himself unattractive, and when this fails he indulges in self-pity.

Completing projects. The native may have an excessive concern with rounding things out, finding balance or finishing things. He feels uncomfortable unless he can tie up all the loose ends and attain closure. On the other hand, he may have trouble with laziness and find it hard to follow through and finish his efforts.

MARS

Mars is the principle of tension, which motivates us to initiate activities and take action. It is an aggressive principle related to the need to take action in support of inner purposes, or in response to social challenge. It is the energy that permits us to function. It indicates desire, which impels us to reproduce. It is the fight or flight factor which assures survival. It allows us to accomplish something in the physical world. Mars difficulties are, therefore, indicators of difficulty in worldly activity.

The Mars inconjunct indicates a disruption of the ability to assert oneself or to take initiative. The aspect tends to either inhibition or excessive aggressiveness. Circumstances seem to preclude the inhibited type from taking initiative, or force him into a passive role. He may also find it difficult to take action or initiative, even when the situation demands it. This behavior stems from parental suppression of his initiative in childhood. He may have been an overactive child, or his parents may have been oversensitive. He may have been punished for his natural aggressiveness. This will result in an inhibition of his natural desire to play, run, jump, climb, fight, etc. He may have been told that he should grow up and stop acting like a child – therefore, don't run, jump, etc.

In a woman's chart, this may mean that she was told that girls shouldn't climb fences or play with the boys. The aspect manifests most strongly in puberty, when young women are admonished to stop being tomboys. They are, thus, conditioned to believe that aggressiveness or physical activity is unfeminine.

This aspect can indicate a difference in health or strength between the person and his peers. During childhood, the native may have been stronger, more agile, more active or better coordinated than others, and received his first experiences of success through physical prowess. This can lead him to try to reproduce these successes through activity.

He may equate success with conquest. This can create a person who tries to gain things through force rather than by negotiation. It may create a brash, contentious individual. As a child he may have seen this kind of behavior in the home. His parents may have permitted him to be aggressive and then used excessive force in suddenly disciplining him. If his parents used aggression or intimidation as a means to achieve their aims, the native may emulate their behavior. This may, in extreme cases, lead to psychopathic behavior. He will have no tolerance for frustration, will be unable to accept minor setbacks, and will resort to violence or intimidation to achieve his ends.

This aspect can also indicate that the native was weak or inactive in childhood. The feeling of weakness can either cause him to give up and remain weak or overcompensate by developing physical prowess. He may then dedicate his adult life to proving his strength or capability.

The Mars inconjunct is active in the charts of people who engage in courageous endeavors, or who are sports enthusiasts. The aspect can be an indicator of a need to test or prove oneself strong, courageous or forceful. This may stem from a childhood in which these individuals were forced to prove their daring and strength, and received approval through such acts.

In other cases, they may have lacked courage or were accused of cowardice. This memory may now goad them to acts or postures of heroism. It may also have the reverse effect and cause them to refuse to test themselves. They may be overly susceptible to the dare: "I dare you!" or "You wouldn't dare!" is all they need to make them attempt things they otherwise wouldn't consider. This, too, may be the result of childhood embarrassment at having to back down when confronted by parents, peers or some external obstacle.

This aspect indicates a tendency toward romanticism. The person yearns for romantic/heroic action, which may, in turn, lead him to forcefully take what he desires. It can manifest as action in defiance of authority figures, or as marriage in the face of strong social opposition.

On a sexual level, it can show up as a Casanova complex. This person may be motivated to prove his sexual prowess through promiscuity. The aspect can sometimes indicate an inability to tolerate sexual frustration, or a tendency to combine sex with violence. This can be the end result of severe sexual repression in childhood. It also might cause the development of a rebellious attitude toward traditional mores. In other cases, the aspect can indicate sexual impotence.

The Mars inconjunct usually indicates difficulty in dealing with anger appropriately. The person with this aspect may assume a belligerent attitude or become extremely angry for minor reasons. The aspect also may indicate a fear of anger, which makes the person timid or inoffensive. Again, this behavior may be traced to childhood roots in which the native was taught to repress anger. The natural childhood tendency to throw an occasional tantrum may have been severely suppressed by over-controlling parents. Perhaps they accused him of injuring them through his expression of anger. The parents themselves may have been uncontrolled or violent. If the parents did not deal with their own anger appropriately, or threw tantrums, the native will certainly have had to curb his anger as a matter of survival.

This aspect can indicate that the parents were child abusers. It suggests that the threat of violence was a constant concern to the native. This can cause the person to either resist physical punishment of his own children, or threaten or batter them.

The aspect might indicate a tendency to batter the spouse or anyone who is vulnerable to such treatment. It can indicate a tendency to draw such treatment toward oneself. In a woman's chart, it might suggest an attraction to men who mistreat her.

The aspect can sometimes indicate a tendency toward depression stemming from a lack of contact with anger. This can be a consequence of living with parents who were depressed. On the other hand, the person with this aspect may have got his way through tantrums or threats of violence when he was a child. If his parents gave in to this intimidation, the native would have learned how to manipulate others through anger or the threat of violence.

The Mars inconjunct suggests that the native was forced to work hard, do chores and suffer play deprivation in childhood. It sometimes indicates child labor. It can indicate a Cinderella complex: the feeling of having to work and do chores while others play. This manifests as the need to prove oneself by working extra hard. This individual may take on extra tasks to set an example for others. The aspect may create a nose-to-the-grindstone attitude. He may find himself having to do most of the work while others relax.

The aspect sometimes indicates the loss of a parent early in life and the subsequent need for the native to become prematurely self-reliant. In any event, the need to prove himself self-reliant or hard-working often permits others to take advantage of him. He can rectify the situation by dropping the need to prove himself. This will force others to assume their fair share of the effort.

At its best, the Mars inconjunct indicates self-reliance, courage and initiative. It indicates an ability to work hard, take risks and stand up for one's principles. This permits the person to take actions that others fear. It can be an aspect of leadership because of the fighting spirit it engenders. It can indicate the person who is willing to fight to the end, even to martyrdom.

It allows the individual to adjust his actions to suit current conditions and get others to consider new ways of doing things. It, thus, permits progress in areas of stagnation. It can be used as a peacemaker aspect in which the native brings conflicting parties together to resolve the quarrel. The aspect can create a fierce competitor, pioneer or adventurer who breaks new ground and who is not afraid to take risks to follow his vision. It allows the native to inspire others through hard work and is, therefore, an aspect of leadership through example.

Summary

Self-assertion and taking initiative. The native may be timid or anxious. He may be forced by circumstances into a passive role. There may be difficulty in expressing anger appropriately, and difficulty in handling frustration. Force or intimidation may be used in order to attain a goal.

Proving one's prowess. These natives desire to prove their strength or courage, may act on dares and exhibit a foolhardy heroism. They may take pains to develop physical prowess. They want to be strong and fearless. Some of these natives may become promiscuous. This allows them to demonstrate their sexual prowess.

Action orientation. The native may be action oriented. He can be impatient or impulsive, favoring immediate and direct action regardless of the circumstances. His tendency to refuse rethinking decisions may lead to rash action.

Romanticism. The native is attracted to the heroic image. He wants to act with power and passion and may become a "knight" looking for a cause. There is a tendency to resist restraints on freedom of action.

Work. These natives may be compulsive workers, expending more energy than everyone else. They want to win recognition through hard work. They may be set in their way and refuse to modify their work methods. They may be confronted with situations which challenge this attitude. Some of these natives have problems with procrastination and may find it hard to initiate new projects.

JUPITER

Jupiter is the principle of expansion and growth. It is an optimistic function related to faith, confidence and success. It encourages risk taking, which leads to exploration of new possibilities and the development of new ventures. It permits us to expand ourselves and our mental horizons through activities such as travel, personal reflection and religious experience. It is the medium through which we come to see ourselves within a larger social perspective. Jupiter difficulties often indicate problems in social progress, personal development and social perspective.

The Jupiter inconjunct indicates a disruption of the growth function. Every organism needs to expand and grow in the natural course of its development. In order to do this, it needs favorable conditions, such as relative freedom and security. It also needs some initial success as a seed for future development. Expansion in human terms includes the physical, mental, emotional and spiritual realms, which implies development of personal consciousness, social consciousness and a philosophy of life.

Disruption of the growth function early in life may result from the parents being oversolicitous or overprotective, thereby denying a child the opportunity to learn through his own mistakes. The growth function may also be disrupted by indifferent parents who force a child to fend for himself.

The Jupiter inconjunct can manifest as a difficulty in social perspective, stemming from an internal feeling of smallness. The internal dynamic is that of the child who is forced to impress others. The aspect motivates the individual to try to make people think highly of him. He may be excessively expansive; he may be overly generous with his money (the big spender); he may give up his space or his knowledge to assist others. This type seems to be saying, "See, I have so much that I can easily afford to let you have some." What he is really saying is, "I want you to think highly of me."

This inconjunct may lead the person to puff himself up to compensate for a sense of inadequacy. He may feel that the only way others will accept him is through an overinflated facade. He dares not show his inner, small self. This facade permits people to prevail upon him for help. He can't say no, because to say no might be an admission of his own needs.

The exact opposite also can occur. The native, although presenting an overinflated facade, will demand all kinds of favors and become outraged if denied. This is the result of being caught between two needs: the need to make childlike demands upon others, and the need to impress them at the same time. This person, rather than being expansive, will be frugal and demand generosity from others. Both of these behavior patterns may also be the result of the threat of poverty in childhood.

The Jupiter inconjunct may indicate self-confidence and personal optimism problems. Self-confidence results from successfully meeting childhood challenges with the interest and support of the parents. A child, by successfully overcoming obstacles and solving new problems, grows to feel that he can rise to the occasion or meet new obstacles successfully. He develops a sense of optimism about his ability to meet the challenges of life. This translates into personal confidence.

If the Jupiter function has been disrupted, personal confidence is damaged. The individual may compensate by trying to prove that he can overcome any obstacle or challenge. Loss of confidence translates into difficulty in making social contacts, missed opportunities or inability to create opportunities. Over-compensation causes rash or opportunistic behavior.

This aspect often expresses itself as a need to impress others. This may be the result of the native having been used by his parents for their own self-aggrandizement. If they boasted of his talents or achievements, he will have felt pressured to live up to their claims or expectations. If his parents prematurely pushed him to expand to the level they demanded, he will feel great insecurity because accelerated expansion leaves an internal void. Early growth and development should be gradual to allow for the full incorporation of each stage in the process.

The native may secretly feel overrated and fear being found out. This can create feelings of superficiality which manifests as dilettante activity or as an intense drive for knowledge. This person may become a collector of knowledge, depending on book learning and citing external authority to support his positions because he lacks faith in his own resources. He feels empty inside, so he tries to fill himself with knowledge or food. The pressure of childhood to live up to being overrated can leave him overextended and vulnerable.

The fear of being discovered can create feelings of hypocrisy, which might make him fear and avoid challenge. He might, then, learn various ways of discouraging confrontation, such as presenting an impressive facade to intimidate others. If he was prematurely pushed and failed, he may have developed a failure complex. If he is a failure, no one will expect things of him and he will not have to live up to their expectations. He might also prevent others from forming high expectations by constant self-deprecation, which may not work, since people tend to interpret this as modesty. What this person really wants is relief from the pressure of other people's expectations.

The Jupiter inconjunct may indicate one who was very underrated in childhood. The experience of being constantly underrated or belittled can create a need to compensate by exaggerating or boasting about one's achievements. This person may feel a need to "toot his own horn" in order to preclude losing opportunities due to being underrated.

This aspect indicates either childhood overprotection or neglect. In the case of neglect, the native may have been left alone or in the care of others while his parents attended to their own interests. This can arouse either a deep fear or an expectation of abandonment.

The abandonment experience profoundly injured the native's ability to be intimate with others. Intimacy implies openness, vulnerability and, therefore, confidence in the other. If your parents abandoned you, what can you expect from others? The experience subsequently creates the expectation that openness and intimacy will be rewarded with abandonment. This belief may turn out to be a self-fulfilling prophecy because he may attract people who flee from him or who are not available for close relationships.

If the abandonment or neglect occurred in very early childhood, the native may have developed the feeling of being among strangers, in an unfamiliar environment. This may have caused him to close up and contract. The primary expansion and growth period may, therefore, have become tainted with anxiety. This may manifest later as anxiety in relation to growth, change or pursuit of new opportunities.

The immediate effect of overprotection or neglect is reflected in a child's learning pattern. When a child is neglected, he has to learn by himself, without the feeling of parental support and the optimism and confidence this creates. If a child is coddled, its growth is stultified through the lack of experience in testing itself at simple tasks. In some cases, the aspect may indicate a sudden shift from pampering to neglect. This may happen either through the birth of a sibling or through some family concern which forces parental attention in another direction.

The Jupiter inconjunct can indicate a severe curtailment of freedom in childhood. This may describe the child who is tied to his mother's apron strings. If he is not permitted to play with his peers and form friendships, he will experience his home as a prison. Close relationships, therefore, can be stifling for him. This may also manifest as a resistance to intimacy in later life.

This aspect can indicate an overconcern for legalistic correctness or a fear of breaking the rules. If one of the parents had some difficulty with the law, it may have created a fear that the parent would be taken away. The parents, if weak, may have threatened the native in order to control him, by telling him that the police would arrest him. If the parents were religious, they may have threatened him by saying that God would punish him.

Some natives may have been brought up in an oppressive religious or ideological atmosphere which stultified growth. These types may, therefore, overreact against all forms of orthodoxy or may function only within the limitations of such orthodoxy. The latter might be threatened by liberal thought. In some families, this aspect may have manifested either as a lack of rules or as an overly severe set of rules.

A need to manage things for others may cause the individual to be attracted to disorganized situations. He may attract people who rely upon him to manage things for them. This may re-enact childhood circumstances in which he had to manage family affairs. Although willing to manage things for others, he will usually do it as a favor, and with unexpressed resentment, which he uses to support a sense of righteousness. He may assume a self-righteous attitude to compensate for the feeling of being used and put upon.

Of course, he may insist upon doing favors for people, whether or not they want it. He then feels abused when they fail to appreciate all that he has done for them. Favor doing is a particular trap for this person. It seems that people constantly prevail upon him for favors, and he has difficulty rejecting unfair approaches. Others seem to take him for granted and assume he won't say no. The reason for this is that he has, through his inability to say no, surrounded himself with favor seekers. This pattern may be related to early life circumstances in which he was forced to put aside his own needs to assist others.

Another manifestation of this aspect is sensitivity to false promises and good intentions. This person may tend to look at life through rose-colored glasses. He sets himself up for disappointment when others don't fulfill their promises. On the other hand, because he finds it difficult to say no, or because he wants to impress others, he may make promises which he cannot fulfill.

The Jupiter inconjunct can indicate a late bloomer. This sometimes happens because the individual has missed the normal stages of development. He is chronologically older than his level of experience and he must spend many years making up for gaps in life experience. He comes into his own in his later years. This can be a wisdom aspect because feelings of inferiority create a drive for experience and knowledge. The aspect also indicates potential for social leadership. The pain of frustrated development becomes a goad to achievement in the later years of life. Society, thus, gets a chance to benefit through this individual's wisdom and maturity. The major challenge to his enjoyment of life is his need to appear upright, and his refusal to risk letting his hair down. If he can do this while making up for lost experiences, he has a possibility of enjoying the later years of his life in achievement, fulfillment, and wisdom. His personal blessings are then shared with society.

This individual has the potential to become a teacher, especially in his later years. He may also be a good executive or manager. There is literary and promotional potential which might find an outlet in advertising or media. He might also find success in the legal profession.

Summary

Problems with generosity. The native either is excessively generous or demands favors from others. He tends to be expansive and wasteful, but sometimes this occurs with other people's possessions or resources. He may be imposed upon to share his physical space with others, and have difficulty saying no.

Impressing others. The native lacks self-confidence and compensates for this by attempting to present an impressive facade. He wants to appear upright. Maintenance of dignity is an important concern for him. He may secretly worry about being found out. A need to save face may force him to forego opportunities.

Lack of perspective. This individual tends to either overrate or underrate himself and others. He expects to be belittled and may jeopardize opportunities because of this. Sometimes, he is overrated and secretly fears being exposed.

Promises and expectations. The native feels pressured to live up to the expectations of others. He tends to overextend himself and make promises he can't fulfill. He may fail in order to defeat the expectations of others. There is a tendency to be somewhat gullible.

Intimacy problems. The native tends to have difficulty getting close to others. He may suffer from fear of abandonment, which may result in clinging behavior. He may attract people with this problem. He may attract people who cannot become close or who are not available. This individual tends to fear entrapment and the compromise of freedom that a close relationship may entail.

SATURN

Saturn symbolizes the principle of concrete reality – teaching the virtues of economy, discrimination and restraint as a key to survival. The Saturn inconjunct indicates disturbances in the reality function. The inception of personal identity, beginning with sensory individuation and the perception of separateness, brings with it an abnormal response to concepts of dependence and/or limitation.

This inconjunct manifests as feelings of limitation and the need to prove oneself responsible. The individual may limit his freedom by assuming responsibilities and burdens. This may indicate the premature assumption of burdens in childhood. The native's parents may have been irresponsible; the native may have had to become a parent to his own immature parents. His parents may have admonished him for being too childish.

This aspect also may indicate a relatively impoverished childhood. The father may have been unwilling or unable to support the family. This may have forced the mother or the native to support the family. During childhood, he may have had to perform household chores, foregoing playfulness in order to assume the worry and burden of family survival.

This experience can create pressure to assume responsibility for others when they fail. It, therefore, permits others to unload their burdens upon this individual. It seems that others enjoy themselves while he is forced to grapple with unpleasant tasks. He thinks that if it weren't for him, everything would fall apart. He comes to resent the tasks he has assumed. Of course, he has surrounded himself with people who are irresponsible. He must become aware of the roots of the pattern if he is to alter this way of life.

This pattern may also result from being the eldest child in a broken family. If the parents separate, the eldest child may be thrust into the position of parent surrogate to his siblings and must prematurely assume adultlike responsibilities. This leads to feelings of deprivation which reflect the reality of being prematurely cast into a grown-up mold.

The feeling of limitation can be traced to circumstances in childhood. If poverty forced someone to wear old clothes or subsist on a meager diet, it may lead to extreme frugality, which might serve him well in some ways, but it also can undermine the ability to enjoy life. The sense of limitation can create a parochial attitude akin to walking around with blinders on. Limited options or resources may force the development of careful planning.

The theme of restriction manifests in clannish, aristocratic or wealthy families. Here, the limitation is one of being a member of a special group. Sometimes the feeling of limitation comes from tradition. The person may be forced to consciously decide either to accept those limitations or take the consequences of rejecting them. This decision is made more difficult because rejection of the restriction may create strong social pressure, which might result in separation from one's class, group or circumstances.

Feelings of limitation are often related to feelings of isolation, loneliness and alienation. The person may find himself alone much of the time. If he was confined in the home or deprived of social contact as a child, he will, feeling self-conscious or socially awkward, find it difficult to be gregarious in social situations. This individual may become an observer instead of a participant, especially if rejected by playmates because of a lack of skills to play.

Feelings of isolation may result from living with lonely and isolated parents. This person may feel guilty for leaving parents to play with friends. Or, parents may have been confining or over disciplined – even making an example of the child. In some cases, the native may have experienced isolation or separateness because of cultural, ethnic or religious differences with neighbors.

The Saturn inconjunct suggests caution and circumspection stemming from a profound sense of anxiety. It makes people either very cautious or just the opposite. This anxiety may be the result of childhood worry about the future, either to avoid harsh discipline or because early life was anxiety laden. The parents may have been constant worriers; perhaps they instilled a "what if" mentality. If the parents were pessimistic, continually focusing upon the most negative possibilities, fear, pessimism or gloom may have been developed.

Inner states of anxiety can also result from the need to prove oneself to fastidious parents who had severe standards, which are continued in adulthood. On another level, this can create someone who is convinced that everyone else has low standards or lacks circumspection. This person can become attached to inept people and try to straighten them out. He will do the worrying for them because they won't or can't do it for themselves.

This aspect suggests an overconcern with realism. The individual can end up in the position of forcing reality into other's lives and projects. Reality might mean greater concern, higher standards, setting limits, more discipline, greater determination, a more serious purpose, etc. This might be needed, but at the same time it may be resented. It might be hard to watch others in their "unreality" without interfering. Of course, "reality" for this person may not be reality at all – it might be merely pessimism.

Caution can translate into hesitancy and inaction. He can frustrate other people's activity (as well as his own) and needlessly discourage them in their aspirations. This can cause them to avoid him or reject his ideas, leaving him unable to apply his experience. They would rather not be told all the reasons why it cannot or should not be done.

If the native's parents discouraged activities by citing tradition, or through general pessimism, this individual might develop a strong opposition to authority or tradition. He may have been told, "That's not the way it's supposed to be done," or, "We've always done it this way," or "What do you know? You're so young." He may now be involved with people who discourage new methods. He may feel stymied by tradition or past experiences, and feel forced to defer to older people or authorities who have their eyes focused firmly on the past.

The Saturn inconjunct indicates problems with time and timing. This person may be forced to be patient or endure delays and restrictions. He may have been forced to wait interminably or was rushed and harried in childhood. This creates frustration (from having to wait) or anxiety (from being rushed). As a child, he may have been rushed when he should have been given time, and given time when he should have been rushed. This can effectively disrupt his natural sense of timing and timeliness. Impatient and restless, he might speak or act prematurely, thus decreasing his effectiveness. In other cases, delay and hesitation might cause him to miss opportunities.

The Saturn inconjunct indicates that authority and respect are major issues in this person's life. He may seek the respect of authority figures, only to be disappointed. He may be forced to pay homage to authorities or tradition. He may be motivated to seek positions which will earn him recognition.

This issue suggests that he was treated with disrespect by his parents. He now tries to earn the respect or acknowledgement of authorities, who withhold it, or may even persecute him. As he achieves success, he may develop a following that regards him with reverence. His supporters may place him on a pedestal regardless of his wishes. After suffering the persecution of his doubters he now must endure the excesses of his supporters.

Other possibilities indicated by the aspect include a concern for structures and defenses. These may, again, be traced to a lack of family structure or behavioral guidance. This individual may be drawn to rigid belief systems or membership in structured organizations. This may indicate a heavily defended person who can sometimes swing to the opposite direction, lose all defenses and become unable to set limits. Knowing this, he may desperately cling to the facade of control to avoid revealing doubt or weakness because of a fear of total collapse.

On the constructive side, this aspect leads to development of inner strength because it forces him to develop and rely on his own resources and authority. The aspect creates an ability to structure events and set limits. It creates a strong sense of responsibility and concern for high standards of quality. It teaches the person about timing, patience, and demands self-discipline. It engenders austerity, economy and efficiency. The aspect pushes the person toward mastery of the illusions of life. Hardship and sorrow help cement his character, provided he also learns how to laugh, especially at himself. The aspect teaches him to accept the fact that he is a human being. This realization qualifies him to fulfill the essential role of teacher.

This individual might find success in traditional businesses, where steadiness and reliability will be valued. Mature demeanor, and a sense of responsibility and restraint, may ultimately lead to positions of authority. Ability to structure work and diminish costs might find fruitful expression in project or industrial engineering activities. This aspect also helps him develop the self-discipline which might lead to mastery of physical pursuits, such as playing a musical instrument or conditioning the body.

Summary

Accepting responsibility. The native wants to prove himself responsible and mature. He may attract immature and irresponsible people. There is a tendency to assume the burdens of others. He may be overconcerned with realism, and tends to be either frugal or miserly.

Excessive caution. The native may be cautious and circumspect, sticks to traditional ways of doing things. He can be too pessimistic or discouraging.

Time. The native often is forced to wait and be patient. Other people make demands on his time, and he may find himself either rushed or delayed. The sense of timing may be disturbed.

Respect. The native wants to be respected. He revers authority figures and desires acknowledgment from them. He finds it hard to take a joke.

Standards. The native measures himself against impossibly high standards and suffers from feelings of inferiority; he becomes anxious about his competence. He may adopt a pseudoscientific manner to alleviate feelings of insecurity.

Loneliness. The native feels separated from others and feels lonely and isolated. There is a tendency to awkwardness in groups and difficulty in making new contacts. Competing with others may be difficult.

URANUS

Uranus is the bringer of independence, the breaker of Saturn's structure. Uranus is the sudden manifestation of something that was developing for a long time relating to steady pressure from the past, caused by the repression of Saturn, and its sudden release. Uranus is the constant tension of fault lines under stress before the earthquake, and it is the sudden rupture and release of that tension to create equilibrium. Uranus is, therefore, the great leveler, the great equalizer. This is implied in its rulership of lighting, which is an equalization of geocosmic electrical potential. Saturn keeps the status quo but Uranus ruptures it. Saturn rules for most of the time but Uranus keeps up a steady pressure until it breaks through to equalize the state of things, sometimes by overcompensating in another area. This is the reason Uranus produces differences and eccentricities. The Uranian is eccentric because he feels compelled to counterbalance the social norm. He feels pressure to be unique and different, especially if it shocks others. The Uranus influence gives a perverse satisfaction in upsetting others and overturning the social norm. This is the personal manifestation of the archetypal energy.

The Uranus inconjunct indicates problems manifesting around the issue of individuality. This native desires to be different, but he also experiences anxiety in relation to his differences. Life circumstances make it evident that he is different from others in some major way. This may lead to personal or social embarrassment because people tend to reject him for his eccentricities. If he tries to hide his differences, he lives in fear of discovery. When his differences are exposed, others react strongly because the differences are based upon the principle of equalization, which often implies revolution. When people discover the Uranian's true self, they are upset because he threatens the established order. People deride him by calling him eccentric or perverse.

This urge to be different sometimes stems from a childhood in which he was told that he was different and was treated differently from others. He may have had physical characteristics which marked him as different. Perhaps he was ridiculed for those differences. Perhaps his parents were perverse or had perverse attitudes toward him. He may have been forced to conform to parental eccentricities. He may have developed idiosyncrasies as a means of rebellion, if he was raised in an oppressive traditional environment. The native, unable to confront the oppression directly, invented new ways of doing things so that he retained a sense of his own individuality. He learned to think and act differently, even as he seemed to conform. He may have occasionally shocked others with different ideas or attitudes. He may, thus, develop into a nonconformist, even in minor matters.

The Uranian is known to be unreliable and inconsistent. One of the most important effects of the Uranus inconjunct is the challenge to the person's inconsistency. To repeat, unreliable and inconsistent behavior results from enforced childhood regimentation. The Uranian child is like the wild animal who resists being tamed. He wants to demonstrate that he has not submitted and that he conforms under protest. He develops this behavior as a means of resistance to domestication. He lives in society in enforced conformance with its mores, but he stands outside in consciousness.

The Uranian temperament tends toward excitement, rebelliousness and anxiety. The inconjunct suggests anxiety in relation to the father. It may run in different directions simultaneously, such as anxiety over absence of father or fear of punishment by father. He may have been forced to submit to authority figures or authoritarian tradition. The native may have experienced rage but was unable to express it. Repression of rage leads to general feelings of anxiety.

The Uranus inconjunct may, therefore, indicate powerful feelings of anxiety which mask equally powerful feelings of rage. The individual may experience this as monstrous feelings – perhaps as a fear of monsters, dreams about monsters, fear of the dark, etc. These feelings are the manifestations of repressed destructive urges, which maintain a constant pressure upon his psyche. He may be afraid of suddenly losing his sanity and releasing his powerful destructive urges. He may experience some of these forces through perverse thoughts or desires. He may be attracted to the bizarre. This is a less threatening displacement of the basic fears.

The Uranus inconjunct may imply sexual difficulty, since gratification requires relaxation. The person may have an "attitude" which he takes into the bedroom. This "attitude" is a defense against the anxiety he feels as a result of the repression of his most powerful urges and the ever present monsters which may be released.

The aspect indicates a tendency toward abstraction and noninvolvement on a feeling level. This becomes essential because contact with feelings calls forth the most deeply repressed and frightening impulses. The individual becomes theoretical, concerns himself with the good of humanity and turns his attention away from personal intimacy. His energies are diverted from the personal to the social; from the biological-emotional to the mental-abstract. The biological energies, thus diverted, force the creative function into mental realms. Emotion is sacrificed for enthusiasm over ideas and abstractions. Biological creation becomes ideational creation.

The person is seen to possess an amazingly fertile and inventive mind. He tends to think abstractly. Ideas and ideals vivify him more than close relationships. People exist as material for his speculations. The more he avoids the emotional-feeling state, the more his biological energies manifest as abstract thought. However, his thinking is usually perverse in at least some respects. It has to be in order to give some release to the monsters within.

Others may see him as odd or eccentric and instinctively fear him. They sense a lack of real feeling. His compassion and love are too impersonal. The Uranian, because of his anxieties, is caught in a bind. He fears intimate relationships because he may suffer abridgement of his individuality and because he fears opening up his inner feelings. But, he is also fearful of being alone (to face the dark) and wants someone to be with him. He may find a solution either by developing an arm's-length intimacy or involving himself with groups instead of individuals.

It is often said that the Uranian temperament is altruistic. There is nothing altruistic about the Uranian inconjunct. This person does not act from love, although he may think he does, but, rather, from anxiety or displaced rage. His good deeds are not based upon love for humanity but are a displacement of his biological urges into the mental, abstract or theoretical. On the surface he may seem to be a "good guy." Buried far below the surface, however is a volcano. He may be so fearful of this volcano that he desperately clings to his nice facade.

As he turns from the biological-emotional toward the mental, his energies turn toward mental creativity instead of biological creativity. He may feel pained at his differences and at his exile from the natural processes of life. However, he soon begins to find ego gratification through recognition by others of his creative and inventive genius. He becomes extremely competitive on a mental level. He can become jealous of others who would usurp his acclaim. He may attack people who threaten to draw attention away from him through superior creativity or inventiveness.

The Uranian can become the inventor who creates technological break-throughs that permit humanity to advance toward mastery over nature. He may be called altruistic but, like the mad scientist, he is actually driven to conquer nature by his rage against it. His inventions are attempts to attack and conquer the limitations nature sets upon its creatures. Since he cannot participate in the natural process, he unleashes the monsters of his psyche in an attack upon nature and creates inventions which turn out to be Frankensteinian in the long run. Technology is the ultimate enemy of nature and, on an unconscious level, the Uranian knows it.

The Uranian invention puts the focus upon machine, which is emotionless and heartless. As inventions improve the quality of life, they also replace nature with machinery. The native's focus upon technology diverts his attention from his inner self. Instead, he projects his monsters outward in the form of invention. Sooner or later, however, he comes to fear this external manifestation as he fears his inner self. He first presents his inventions as emancipators of humanity, but soon begins to feel the need for emancipation from the technology he has created.

The native, driven by unconscious rage, is motivated to "enlighten" others. He does this by exposing the truth in the most upsetting way, in order to shock people into realization. The actual desire is not so much to inform as to shake and turn upside down. He desires to shatter the norm or that which is taken for granted. This may have immense social value, but it can be devastating in close relationships. It adds yet another barrier between himself and others. People tend to avoid close involvement with him rather than submit themselves to a continual shock treatment. This person wants to psychically assault others, regardless of his outer expression. He may do this quietly or loudly, but it is still the same.

The desire to shake and dislodge can be expressed through shocking ideas, sudden exposure of disquieting information, perverse acts, "black" humor, etc. The Uranus inconjunct can create quite a revolutionary who wants to disrupt societal norms. In order to make an omelette, you have to crack a few eggs; in order to attain the revolutionary aim you may have to crack a few million heads. As the idea becomes more real, people become more abstract. This revolutionary is likely to maintain an amoral stance, disposing of all who stand in the way (as opposed to his way) of the ultimate goal. He is likely to resort to extreme measures to suppress competitive ideologies. Should his revolution succeed, he is capable of initiating ruthless measures to bring about his ideal concept.

The Uranian is often considered an emancipator. In the inconjunct, this is true only in the sense that he wishes to emancipate people from their current conditions. The real drive is to turn things upside down. In opposition to oppression and tyranny, he becomes an emancipator. However, the aspect can just as easily manifest as the desire to overthrow democracy, where it is the prevailing condition. Facing a democratic system, he may wish to overturn it in favor of tyranny; facing religious oppression, he might wish to overturn it in favor of secularism; facing a secular system, he may wish to overturn it in favor of theocracy. In any event, the Uranian is guided by his vision and takes little account of how people actually feel.

In its positive manifestations, this inconjunct indicates brilliance of intellect. It generates enormous creative power which shatters boundaries and opens new vistas. It creates high aspirations and causes one to embark on new and unique ventures. The Uranian has a gift for the world and it is through his individual struggles that the world benefits from his genius. He is often ahead of his time and he serves to sow the seeds for humanity's future development.

The aspect drives one to return to first principles and, thus, rethink or reinvestigate things, starting with the basics. The possibility of social illumination is, therefore, created in the clash between the Uranian and his society. It is created by the challenge at the root level. As he attempts to uproot the established society, that society is forced to reconsider its basic premises and is given the opportunity to modify its processes.

This aspect might find useful application in development of new methodology. This person may be excellent in creative or artistic fields. His talent for abstract thought and problem solving might make him good at trouble shooting. He is good at one-of-a-kind projects. He might also make a good investigative reporter.

Summary

Individuality. The native has strong urges to be different. Because others tend to inhibit his individuality, he may be forced to suppress his differences and conform.

Anxiety. The native may suffer from high levels of anxiety. Anxiety is created in others through the unpredictability of his actions and the perversity of his thoughts. He likes to shock people to make his point.

Rebelliousness. The native tends to have high levels of unconscious rage. He may present a mild exterior which masks his deeper feelings. He wants to overturn things.

Abstract thinking. The native tends to be creative on a mental level. He thinks abstractly and attacks problems at their roots. He thinks in terms of the basics. He can be intellectually competitive and may feel threatened by other creative people.

NEPTUNE

The Neptune function relates to the prenatal state and the early period of infancy. It is a realm where sight, sound, smell, touch and taste all merge. It is a world where everything is equivalent to everything else. It is a world of formlessness and timelessness; a world without points of reference. Neptune is the indicator of the greater world, in which the Saturnian world of "reality" is but a small part. In metaphorical terms, Saturn is the island realm within the great Neptunian ocean. The Saturn realm is stable, limited and bounded by time and space, whereas Neptune's realm is boundless, infinite and protean. In Neptune's world, everything is simultaneously possible. The Neptunian is capable of being in several places at once, whereas the Saturnian is not. The Saturn-Neptune interaction forms the border at which things simultaneously are and are not what they are. On the Saturn side, things are what they are. On the Neptune side, everything can be everything else.

The Neptunian finds it difficult to live in Saturn's realm. He is a foreigner, a fish out of water. He becomes frustrated at the tremendous restriction of his free-flowing nature. He little realizes, however, just how much he threatens the Saturnian. The latter is at home on a small island in a threatening sea, and the former continually reminds him of it. The Neptunian can swim in his ocean. He belongs there. The Saturnian must cling to his very carefully built raft. The Saturnian is terrified of the Neptunian realm and tries to reduce it to his own terms. This creates a problem for the Neptunite, who is trying to live in Saturnia without being stultified.

Neptune governs the ability to think creatively. It permits us to break the bounds of currently accepted reality and explore new vistas. In order to live in Saturnville, we must all, to some extent, wear blinders and govern ourselves according to structured rules. This permits us to know what to expect from others. However, the world is much greater than we are consciously aware. We are parochial and it is Neptune's function to bring us intimations of those other dimensions of life.

If Neptune is functioning well, the person can readily integrate these awarenesses into life. The inconjunct makes this difficult because the aspect frequently manifests as fantasy and illusion. The individual may act inappropriately due to his inability to see things realistically. He may act according to fantasy or illusion, with disastrous results, or refrain from acting and daydream instead. Daydreaming is different from illusion because the daydreamer, at least, can tell the difference between fantasy and reality. The person acting under an illusion mistakes fantasy for reality.

The tendency to live in fantasy may come from childhood experiences of being profoundly hurt and disappointed. This native, therefore, turned to fantasy in order to assuage his inner pain. If reality was too painful, he may have developed strong wish-fulfillment fantasies. He may grow to adulthood trying to live out his fantasies by projecting them onto others.

This aspect often manifests as confusion due to giving and receiving of double messages. The native tends to give conflicting signals. Others do not know what he means or wants. He may not know either. He also tends to attract people who give double messages, which may reflect an inner ambivalence. He wants something but, simultaneously, doesn't want it. This may mirror childhood experiences in which he either was forced to retreat from his desires or had to show a false interest. His parents may have given him double messages so that he didn't know what to expect or how to act.

This aspect also manifests as vacillation or fickleness. He isn't sure of what he wants. He may be unable to make a commitment. He may attract people who are fickle toward him. This behavior may reflect a childhood with fickle parents. Parental vacillation will have created great uncertainty in him. He may be fickle toward others but he becomes pained at any ambivalence towards him.

He needs a great deal of reassurance and despairs at the slightest nuance of disapproval. He tends to be plagued by self-doubt and finds it difficult to assess himself realistically. He depends upon continual positive feedback from others to help bolster his wavering self-esteem. He doubts others' love and respect for him, too. This ultimately puts such a strain upon relationships that his greatest fears come true. He may involve himself with people who relate to him for ulterior motives, who use him and then discard him. He secretly expects this and, therefore, finds it hard to trust others. When the rejection occurs, he feels vindicated in his self-doubt. He may be easy to deceive because he so desperately needs reassurance.

In some cases, this aspect may indicate that the native was victimized by a hoax or made the butt of a practical joke. He tends to oppose kidding and has a sympathy for the victim. This makes him very sensitive to the whole issue of trust, deceit, deception or hypocrisy. It can create a compulsive truth teller or, in some cases, a trickster.

The Neptune inconjunct can indicate difficulty in concentration. The person may be absent-minded, or easily distracted. He may forget, lose or misplace things. He can be careless and irresponsible. He may appear aimless or lacking in direction. He may have been distracted as a child, or learned to emulate these characteristics in his parents. He may also have developed this behavior as a reaction to threatening circumstances. Perhaps it was an early show of resistance against overbearing authority.

Absentmindedness and inability to concentrate may also indicate a tendency to drift off into fantasy, a form of behavior related to escapism. If reality is too difficult or painful, one attains some satisfaction or relief through fantasy. Of course, if fantasy is insufficient, the person may seek escape through alcohol or drugs. This aspect, thus, indicates the possibility of using drugs or alcohol as escapist relief valves.

Issues of obligation can also be a part of this inconjunct. The native either may be obligated to others or avoid obligations. He may avoid relationship for fear of becoming obligated. Once he accepts an obligation, however, he finds it almost impossible to shake it off. This behavior comes from childhood circumstances in which he was expected to accept responsibilities or chores, while at the same time being taken for granted. He may have initially refused to accept responsibilities but was slowly made to feel guilty over it. After a while, he became more responsible. He grows up volunteering for the tasks that others refuse, and may become so sensitive about being taken for granted that he can refuse obligations.

Obligation means promises to take responsibility in the present or future. In many ways, this is like a combination of Jupiter and Saturn inconjuncts. The whole issue revolves around the promise and the responsibility; the giving up of time and opportunity and the need for reliability. Also involved are generosity and maturity, wanting others to think well of you and the desire to be respected. Obligation brings up issues of self-righteousness, pride and self-respect. The people on the other side of the issue often do not appreciate your actions or sacrifices. They, rather, expect it from you. The person under the obligation believes he is acting morally or ethically. He is motivated by a strong sense of ought, which comes from early life conditioning. The sense of obligation brings with it the feeling that others are depending on him or that failure to discharge his obligations will profoundly affect others' lives.

The Neptune inconjunct can indicate extreme impressionability or suggestibility. These people may lack the inner structure that certainty gives, and this makes them malleable. Uncertainty makes them open to suggestion. A compassionate nature allows others to play on their feelings. Vulnerability, in this case, may stem from parents who needed too much sympathy.

The challenge of the Neptune inconjunct is to dissolve the rigid structures of Saturn. On its highest levels, it is the dissolver of divisive egoism. It points the way, through mystical vision, to common origins. This aspect permits us to touch the deepest wellsprings within us. We become aware of these potentialities through dreams, visions and mystical feelings. The Neptune inconjunct is the divine discontent which makes us restless and forces us to seek the solitude which nurtures our inner nature. On a superficial level it may manifest as escapism. On spiritual levels it indicates the possibility of confronting our inner wellsprings and coming in touch with the infinite. The Neptunian, therefore, has a great gift to give us, provided that he does not so lose himself in his vision that he cannot function in the "real" world.

This aspect indicates a potential talent for art, music, dance, poetry or mystical vision. The individual may find great satisfaction in religious pursuits or in service to others. His visual and imaginative abilities may find application in photographic pursuits or other visual arts. Success may also be found in travel or entertainment industries.

Summary

Obligations. Obligation becomes a major issue in this native's life. He either accepts unwanted obligations or adamantly refuses them. He may feel pressured to make sacrifices.

Creative thinking. The native has the ability to think imaginatively, visually and imagistically. There may be mystical or visionary tendencies.

Idealism. The native can be highly romantic with unrealistic ideals which lead to disillusionment. He creates problems for himself through his inability to see others clearly.

Vagueness. The native may be vacillating and ambivalent. Double messages and ulterior motives (his own and those of others) create problems for him. Self-doubt and uncertainty create additional problems. His need for reassurance may undermine the confidence of others in him. He tends to be impressionable and too open to deception.

Escapism. The native may engage in excessive fantasy or daydreaming. He may be absent-minded or have difficulty concentrating, and is prone to mistakes and errors. He may turn to drugs or alcohol for escape from his burdens.

PLUTO

Pluto represents the function of elimination – getting rid of the old and useless, and expelling dead material which no longer serves any purpose. The Pluto function serves to cleanse us by ejecting material before it begins to decay and rot. The elimination of decayed matter keeps the body fresh and healthy. The body is cleansed and room is made for new material to be absorbed. On another level, Pluto rules the decay and disintegration of eliminated matter. Organic matter, excreted by animal life, returns to the earth where it is decomposed to form the nutriments necessary for the nourishment of plant life, which, in turn, provides the nourishment of animal life. The Pluto function literally allows life to continue. It is an essential part of nature's plan for mutual interaction and eventual cooperation of varying life forms.

On the human level, elimination can be expanded to mean letting go: letting go of old feelings, old ideas, old practices, etc. This is the ultimate mental hygiene. Outworn ideas turn the mind stale and prevent us from thinking or perceiving freshly. If we wish to be alert and alive, we must eliminate stale thoughts, emotions, ways of doing things, in order to make way for the new. The Pluto inconjunct indicates difficulties in this area.

One tends to hang on to the past and obsess over things. This ultimately results in fear of change. The biological effect of the blocked or disturbed Pluto function is constipation or diarrhea. On a mental level, this means obsessing over old ideas, inability to express feeling, inability to change methodology, etc. Mental constipation inhibits living in the present. Mental diarrhea means an inability to tolerate anything new.

The Pluto inconjunct manifests as diarrhea or constipation in regard to the specific planetary function. For example, the Mercury-Pluto inconjunct might lead either to silence, reserve, or to compulsive talking; the Mars-Pluto inconjunct might lead to persistence in outmoded methods or an inability to stick to a particular method; the Moon-Pluto inconjunct might indicate holding on to old feelings, emotional reserve, or extreme emotionality.

The individual with this aspect may be extremely neat, make a big fuss over neatness, or he may be sloppy and disorderly. These behaviors indicate premature or severe toilet training. If the parents were too severe, the native may have become anxious over their displeasure. His attempts at control are connected to avoidance of failure in bowel control. This aspect can also indicate childhood problems with bed wetting. When this occurs, the child may be humiliated by those who would train him to control himself. This wound may manifest as the need to be neat (not soil himself) or maintain control. It may also manifest as sloppiness or inability to maintain control.

The issue of control is usually very important to this person. The need to control causes the following kinds of behavior: The individual may try to maintain control of situations and people; he may also be manipulative or the victim of manipulative people. He may appear to others as having a power complex, for inner needs to control – and a fear of loss of control – are often viewed as that. The behavior may also be traced to the parental environment. If he has controlling and manipulative parents, he may emulate this behavior. If his parents are weak and gullible, the individual may learn to manipulate his parents and other people in order to get what he wants. This manifests in adult behavior as one who pays attention to details to attain the effects he desires – he learns how to use appearance, words, emotions, actions or threats to manipulate or control others. His ability to learn to discern and satisfy others' needs ultimately makes him a master of the art of diplomacy and guile.

Pluto inconjunct people tend to be very analytical. This is another manifestation of the need to control. Analysis involves breaking things apart, sorting them out and putting them together again in order to understand the inner workings. This results in the knowledge which leads to power and control. The problem is that when one is too analytical, one is too controlled. Somewhere in the breakdown and reconstruction, the inner spark is lost. Similarly, an overanalytical nature leads to the loss of spontaneity.

The Pluto inconjunct indicates obsessions. The native may be driven to hold on to people, ideas, feelings, money, work habits, etc. This may be the result of painful losses in childhood. Obsession is an indirect way of asserting will and experiencing some power. The natives fixes on the object of obsession and refuses to let go because he fears loss, or because he fears the present life situation. This behavior may result from the need to fixate on something in order to avoid the pain of the present. It implies that the individual went through much profound pain. On the other hand, this person may find himself entangled by obsessive and clinging people. This is a re-enactment of a childhood with obsessive or clinging parents.

This aspect is sometimes felt as the need to change or reform ideas, things or people. This gives a feeling of power over the person or thing. The native asserts himself by eliminating things or qualities he doesn't like, and replacing them with those he prefers. Sometimes it is the opposite:

He may attract people who wish to change or reconstruct him. This reflects early life experiences of a similar nature. He seems unwilling to accept people as they are. There is a desire to recreate things to fit his ideal images.

Individuals with this inconjunct may dwell upon systems within which to categorize people. They are, in essence, trying to attain some feeling of control and stability in a world they view as chaotic. The conceptualization of the world within a system creates a feeling of order, a sense of certainty about life, and security in a world which might otherwise be frightening due to a lack of control over it. They, thus, find meaning in life and a sense of connectedness to the world. They see themselves as part of a system, which gives them a sense of rightness in action. This attitude is evident in their behavior. They seem to speak and act with certainty. This impresses others who are seeking some system within which to view life, and who also wish to feel some control in life. People want to perceive some purpose to life and, therefore, to their own lives. These natives are, therefore, prone to becoming the creators or followers of a doctrine by which they identify themselves.

This native defends the system he has adopted and is intolerant of the views of others. This behavior betrays a fear of uncertainty. The need for certainty creates a desire to know how to act, what to do or what may be expected. These people fear the unexpected and, thus, constantly think about the future. They want to know how things will turn out before they even get started. They want to know what others are thinking, and they may question others in detail about their intentions.

This need leads to difficulties because others cannot tolerate the native's third-degree treatment. He tends to make others feel suffocated because, on an inner level, he wants to capture and preserve them so that he may possess them forever, as they now are. He wants to avoid the unexpected at all costs because it is perceived as threatening.

He is concerned about being correct at all times. He may be prone to conform to things he reads in books or the views of authorities. Relationships are squelched by his attempt to relate according to pre-conceived notions. It is essential to let go of this need if he is to find any satisfaction in relationships.

This aspect gives the potential for understanding the deeper meanings of things. This native has a potential talent for research, analysis and diplomacy. He may have a knack for modifying or reforming things. He might make a good actor, salesperson or psychologist. If he learns how to let go of outworn perceptions, he can grow spiritually by living in the now.

Summary

Obsessiveness. The native may have difficulty letting go of old feelings, ideas, practices, etc. He tends to be obsessive and attracts obsessive people. There may be an inability to assimilate new ideas, feelings, etc. He may either become clinging and dependent or attract clinging people.

Control. The native may be manipulative and controlling, and may attract manipulative or controlling people. He can be overly analytical and tends to lack spontaneity. He may be either excessively neat or sloppy. A desire to change or reform the people or situations around him can be strong.

Certainty. The native has a great need for certainty and a great fear of uncertainty. He wants to be absolutely certain that he is thinking or acting correctly. He wants to know what others are thinking or doing and may question people incessantly, allowing them no peace. He may be very doctrinaire, and may try to live according to agendas.

The Angles

Each hour approximately 15,000 souls come off the production line into the world. Their birthcharts are essentially the same but for the angles (the Ascendant-Midheaven relationship). Births occur over 24 time zones and some 120 degrees of latitude. This means that there are only a few hundred people in the world with the same horoscope. The angles of the chart, are, thus, important in defining individuality within the collective.

The Ascendant-MC (1st and 10th houses) relationship defines the planetary house locations and, therefore, individuality by indicating the specific areas of life to which the planetary energies will be brought to bear. Within this overall picture, the Ascendant indicates the personal style, while the MC indicates social function. (The Sun indicates purpose or intention – who you are; the Moon indicates self-image – the way you react to others or expect others to react to you, based upon past memories – who you think you are. The Ascendant is the impression you make, but the Moon is what you feel like. Personal style includes such things as physical appearance, personality and characteristic manner of expression. Social function includes career, social status and work to be done. The Ascendant-MC relationship provides us with our vehicle in the world. Our task is to learn how to utilize this vehicle most effectively.

The Ascendant-Descendant (1st and 7th houses) axis is the personal/interpersonal axis. It provides the means of self-fulfillment through self-expression on both an impersonal and intensely personal basis. The challenge here is to be an individual, develop a personal style, and at the same time learn to modulate individualistic tendencies through close relationship with another person. This means learning to accept others' personal style and individuality.

The MC/IC (10th and 4th houses) axis is the public-private axis. It defines the native's ventures in the world and his return home for rest and recuperation. The challenge here is to modulate the need for adventure and achievement by developing roots which provide a source of inner strength and spiritual nourishment. Within this framework, the native must find a way of realizing his solar purpose. This means that he must resolve any conflicts between the Sun, Moon and angles.

Aspects of the planets to the angles provide a final customizing influence by accentuating or inhibiting certain qualities. This makes a particular Ascendant or MC different from others of the same type. It is up to the native to resolve the conflicts and inconsistencies in the chart so that he fulfills his solar purpose in the most satisfying and productive way.

Ascendant/Descendant Inconjuncts

The inconjunct of a planet to the Ascendant-Descendant axis emphasizes or exaggerates that planetary function. Issues centering around the function tend to characterize the individual. This function becomes predominant in his consciousness and tends to define his most important concerns, affecting how he wishes to present himself or how others perceive him. The planetary function also defines the most important concern in his relationships. It describes his basic appearance or manner, what he accentuates or plays down. The aspect indicates areas of maximum and minimum compromise, the qualities of which he is most uncertain, and, therefore, either compensates for or represses. The aspect indicates unwillingness to yield, change, reconsider or compromise. The inconjunct to this axis tends to create ingrained, obsessive, stubborn attitudes or behavior. The issue seems to involve maintenance of personal identity. The native seems to fear loss of identity if he should give up his mannerisms.

Planets inconjunct the ASC/DSC axis tend to create disorder in personal expression and interpersonal relationships. The disrupted planetary function takes on great personal significance and describes the manner in which the person feels unique or different from his fellows. The aspect describes the area of life in which he feels most frustrated and dissatisfied. It also indicates where he feels most compromised, or feels the most pressure to compromise himself. It suggests areas of awkwardness and unnaturalness that become the ways in which the person feels set apart from others, and define his sense of personal handicaps and strengths.

This inconjunct indicates a problem centering around being understood. There is a tendency toward excessiveness and redundancy. This behavior may stem from childhood repression. The native may have been forced to explain himself to people who would not listen, and may now attract people who do not understand or will not listen. He may become involved with people who make him feel stifled, or he may avoid relationships because he expects them to be stifling.

This aspect indicates areas of repression, inhibition or unease. Since it also indicates areas of personal uncertainty, it tends to reveal the qualities the person will be most fascinated by or drawn to in a potential partner. It indicates essential qualities that the individual most requires for self-completion. This person may be tempted to manipulate partners to conform to his ideal. The aspect, therefore, indicates where he will not accept people as they are, and what interferes with real intimacy. It may indicate the bogus issues which tend to dominate his life, for these issues define concessions that he must make in order to maintain a relationship.

Also indicated are attitudes about relationship and partnership formed as a reaction to the parents' relationship with the grandparents. It indicates that the native was distressed by his parents' attitudes toward their parents or toward authorities. The aspect is indicative of the neurotic dynasty: neurosis passed down from generation to generation. It defines the need to break free from the neurotic dynasty. This attempt is sometimes made with the help of a partner who challenges or recreates the issues. The native is, thus, prone to choose partners who permit him to recreate the issue.

This aspect indicates illusions which must be dispelled before real relationship is possible. This means that the individual is attracted to people who conform to his illusions. He also attracts people who harbor illusions about him. In either case, there is an expectation which results either in mistrust, anxiety or disappointment. He must learn to overcome these illusions or live with the pain resulting from the refusal to perceive others as real people.

This inconjunct sometimes indicates sentiments about parenthood, which strongly influence his feelings about relationship. This can lead to problems related to the issue of having children. The native may strongly desire to have children while attracting partners who are unable or refuse to have children. The reverse is also possible. The person who rejects parenthood may become involved with a partner who desires children. In any event, he may have problems in his relationships until he comes to terms with how he actually feels about having children. He may, thus, find himself trapped in a relationship which breeds resentment, either because he feels deprived of children or he feels trapped in parenthood. In the latter case, there is a danger of passing these feelings on to his children.

Planets inconjunct the ASC/DSC may indicate sexual attitudes picked up from the parents. One of the parents may have had sexual feelings toward the native, which were either repressed or openly exhibited. The native, perceiving this, might feel upset or confused. He might think this a product of his own fantasies and feel ashamed or guilty. The aspect also indicates possible feelings of discomfort or awkwardness in the parents, as a consequence of his growth toward sexual maturity. He may have internalized these feelings and developed a discomfort toward his own growing sexuality. This aspect may, therefore, indicate the defenses that the person developed in order to cope with this problem.

This inconjunct indicates a tendency for the parents to have related on a childlike level, presenting a form of sibling rivalry to the native. This can be very threatening, and, as a result, the native may have been forced to repress his natural qualities or functions. These repressed functions are difficult to regain because sibling rivalry with the parent can create tremendous feelings of inferiority and fear. The repressed functions are tinged with extremely high levels of anxiety because repression was a matter of survival. He, therefore, clings to this current behavior on a survival level.

This aspect sometimes manifests as a basic discontent that makes partnership difficult. These people drive potential partners away through criticism, and then complain about their loneliness. Actually, they prefer to be alone because a relationship requires too much of a sacrifice (giving up the complaining). Many with this aspect keep their discontent to themselves and attract people who complain. The entire issue suggests that these individuals grew up in an atmosphere of nagging and complaining, especially about money. The aspect also may indicate an uncomfortable attitude about money, which can interfere with partnership.

The inconjunct to the ASC/DSC may permit the native to work well with other people. He has the potential for helping others change, and overcome problems in relationship. He learns to adjust to the challenges that life throws his way and eventually achieves a life of moderation and balance. He is then able to help others bring their lives into greater balance. This aspect finds fruition in such areas as relationship counseling, financial counseling and divorce law. It may also find success as a teacher or therapist. This individual comes to discern the real from the bogus issues in life, permitting him to eventually relate to others in a simpler, more open manner.

Summary

Obsessive behavior. The native is prone to obsessive behavior. He feels different from other people and identifies himself by his idiosyncrasies. He is resistant to change because it may threaten his identity.

Self-expression. The native tends to have difficulty in expressing the planetary function appropriately. He feels awkward and uncomfortable, and tends toward excess and redundancy.

Relationship. The native finds it difficult to accept people as they are. He may harbor illusions about potential partners, or he may attract people who use him as a screen for their illusions. He may attempt to live vicariously through partners, or he may attract people who try to live vicariously through him. He may be forced to make concessions to his opponents and may have to make compromises in order to save his relationships.

Attitudes. The person may feel uncomfortable with his sexuality. He may feel malcontented and can attract complainers. He may feel uneasy in regard to money matters.

Midheaven/Imum Coeli Inconjuncts

Planets inconjunct the MC/IC axis indicate a great deal of inner turmoil. The individual tends to be emotional and frustrated. Some natives are able to express these feelings openly through their activities, while others internalize them.

This native has an attitude toward authority and established conditions which can be described as ambivalent rebelliousness. He opposes authority but isn't sure of what he really wants. He wants to force the world to make concessions, yet also wants permission from the world. This is an essentially childlike condition: He wants permission to be rebellious. He has a strong desire for freedom, yet he cannot disassociate from the restrictions of internalized authority. He seems to be battling against a powerful superego. In some people, this may develop into the age-old struggle between good and evil.

The individual feels a need to ask others for permission to act, and feels resentment over having had to make unfair compromises in childhood. He may have been denied the right to be a child by parents who controlled or obstructed his play. Perhaps he had little playful contact with his parents or siblings. Perhaps he was kept from playing with other children. The joy was taken out of his childhood somehow, and this may have led him to harbor resentment and develop a resentful child subpersonality.

He may provoke people by going to unreasonable limits. Each time he experiences restraint, he re-experiences his childhood resentment, and he attracts or creates these circumstances over and over again. The mere suggestion of any form of denial rekindles childhood bitterness or resentment. Some natives experience exasperation rather than resentment. Their repressed feelings may also manifest as rebellion against authorities. In some cases, the buried emotion may be acted out through coldness toward, or disassociation from, the native's parents. The person feels stuck. He wants to act freely but finds himself struggling against the yoke of early life disappointments.

He can liberate himself by becoming acutely aware of his internalized resentful child, accepting it, and then striving to resolve the issues involved. In the process, he must re-experience his frustration and anger, express it and then let go of it. He will ultimately have to forgive his parents, in the present, for their actions in the past.

The aspect indicates a potential conflict between career and family. The native may have to choose between career ambition and family obligations or may deny family needs in order to further his career. Perhaps his work pulls him away from his family. Some natives may avoid developing a family life because a higher priority is put on career. Family considerations may also be sacrificed to further social status. This may parallel early life deprivation of contact with parents who placed work or social status before family, and may imply a form of revenge against the parents. The issues, however, are thoroughly confused. He has inverted his anger, identified with the disappointing parent and acts out against himself or his family.

This native grows to adulthood and may attain some degree of worldly success, but the resentful child still remains arrested within. He, therefore, continues to be motivated by childlike concerns. Given a degree of power, he might begin to exhibit the characteristics of a dominating child: He may dominate and manipulate others through impatience or petulance. He tends to compare himself with people of achievement and is secretly competitive with them. Before he attains power, he may back down, like a child, when confronted. However, when he does achieve power, he may become very difficult to deal with. He can become a petty tyrant.

As his repressed child comes out, others become concerned. When they oppose him, he becomes even more defensive. He has trouble accepting criticism, and shows his resentful side. The more he is challenged, the more tyrannical he becomes, and the more opposition he creates. He, thus, creates a crisis in his capacity to lead.

This aspect can indicate the possibility of becoming a self-destructive achiever. The native works and sacrifices for the opportunity to achieve, only to undermine himself afterward. This aspect may also operate in the reverse manner, so that this person may deny himself achievement out of a combination of anxiety, self-punishment or spite. Meanwhile, he resents others who are not denying themselves. If the internal child is overwhelmed by fear or awe, he may become anxious or fearful when meeting people he respects. He may collapse under minor criticism and revert to feeling like a powerless child. He may use all kinds of excuses to avoid achievement. He is reluctant to accept his grown-up status and take responsibility for his own fulfillment.

There may be a tendency toward vacillation and indecisiveness. This creates problems in making or sticking to decisions. In some cases, the person may rigidly stick to decisions because he fears reconsideration may throw him into indecision. (These descriptions, of course, concern people who have not come to terms with their inner child. If the person has resolved this, he has the potential of developing an ability to make adjustments which take many factors into consideration. He develops the capacity for enlightened and compassionate leadership.)

This inconjunct often indicates a great concern with personal privacy. The native may become a closed individual who keeps his thoughts and feelings strictly to himself. He may be thrust into situations where others pry into his personal affairs. Authorities may demand to know details of his private life. He may become sensitive and suspicious, fearing that others are spying or gossiping about him. He tries to keep his private life to himself, but, every so often he reveals little details which others are alert to catch.

The aspect also raises the issue of public vs. private life. This person must decide which is more important to him, public achievement or privacy. The aspect can make it difficult to have both, for there is a tendency to lose personal privacy with the attainment of worldly success. The more he attempts to hide his personal life, the more gossip he engenders. This may replay his childhood relationship with the family. He may have had very little privacy. Perhaps his parents spied on him, read his mail or eavesdropped on his conversations; or siblings may have spied and reported back to his parents. Any of these factors may have sensitized him against compromise of personal privacy.

Some of these people may, however, snoop or pry into the private lives of others. They become fascinated by other people's private affairs either through a sense of personal identity with them or because of voyeuristic curiosity. The latter may be the result of frustration of natural curiosity about their parents' lives (especially sex lives). It suggests that their parents may have shared too little of themselves. They may have felt pushed away by their parents' overconcern with privacy, and may now express this curiosity through interest in others.

This aspect also indicates a desire to confront established authorities, or the world at large, with the need to re-examine, reconsider or make adjustments. The individual may be interested in changing the world or forcing it to take account of his criticisms. He has a critical view of conditions. He is dissatisfied with the trend of events. He has a strong sense of the past. This aspect may have useful career application in the field of reporting. The native may use his natural curiosity to examine the affairs of public figures and throw light upon their activities. He may be an historian or researcher.

Perhaps he sees himself speaking for others who are oppressed and resentful. This is a form of transcendancy for the resentful child within. The resentful child no longer speaks only for himself but identifies with the mass of resentment in the world and gives voice to it. The native finds satisfaction by merging with a more universal concern and championing others. He develops a philosophy and a sense of history. He forces authorities to examine their past actions. He challenges the accustomed beliefs of conservative or traditional people. He may be seen as a radical by authorities or defenders of tradition. If frustrated, he may become a revolutionary. If he persists, he may ultimately win the respect of those who most strongly oppose his views.

Summary

Ambivalent rebelliousness. The native tends to be frustrated. He is rebellious but wants permission to rebel. He wants to act but there is a tendency to create or attract situations which force him to restrain himself.

Internalized authority. The native is dominated by a powerful superego. He often is forced to make concessions to parents, tradition or authorities. He finds it difficult to be playful.

Internalized resentment. The native may harbor a great deal of resentment and tends to be motivated by childlike concerns. He may feel trapped, burdened or encumbered.

Career vs. family. The native may be torn between career and family considerations. He may find it hard to make the compromises required for family fulfillment or career success. He may feel a need to prove himself to parents or authorities, or may be forced to submit to authority figures.

Personal privacy. The native wants to keep his thoughts and feelings to himself. Others seem to pry into his private affairs, or he may pry into the private affairs of others.

Changing the world. The native wants to confront society in order to make it re-examine conditions. He wants to force the world to concede to his views. There is a tendency to champion the oppressed.

PART TWO
Planetary Combinations

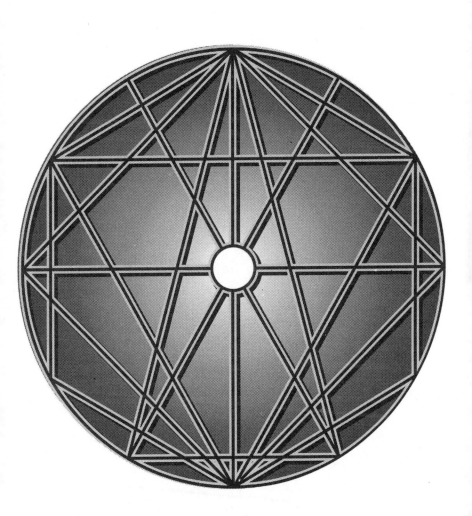

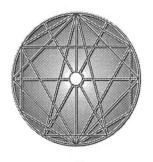

Planetary Combinations

Introduction

ASTROLOGY IS A COMPLEX STUDY. There is no real substitute for careful analysis. The aspects given here only indicate tendencies. Nothing is cast inconcrete. Everything must be considered against the background of the chart as a whole. These aspects will reinforce or minimize other tendencies inherent in the chart. A Pisces/Leo inconjunct may be quite different from a Pisces/Aquarius inconjunct. The planets respond to the aspect according to the signs they are in. The task is to understand the principle of the aspect, and then to determine how the planet will act in that sign or house.

These aspects are general principles. They will describe characteristics of the person. If they do not, then they will surely describe the important people in his life. The basic idea is: either he expresses these qualities or attracts someone who does.

This section contains an introductory exploration of each planetary combination. The material is presented in three sections: The introductory paragraphs give a general overview; the middle sections indicate potential problem areas and major issues; the final paragraph explores potential vocational areas, if the problematic issues can be resolved. Keep in mind that the material covers a range of possibilities. Not everything is valid for each individual. In addition, careful consideration will reveal many possibilities not mentioned. Remember that inconjunct refers both to the quincunx and semisextile. You might review Part I to understand the motivation for each aspect manifestation.

Please note the aspects are listed in order from the Sun to Pluto. For example, to look up a Pluto/Jupiter inconjunct, see Jupiter/Pluto.

SUN INCONJUNCT MOON

The theme here is self-acceptance. These natives are learning to be more tolerant, express feelings and stand up to social pressure. They are challenged to stop seeking approval, overcome the fear of rejection and forego the inclination to judge others.

This aspect puts the emphasis upon human relations. These natives are skeptical and pseudoscientific. They are developing an emotional sensitivity to others and learning to take other people's feelings into account. They make loyal but judgmental friends, and can be very supportive in a crisis. They make life difficult by resisting their own inner needs. Self-acceptance is the key to their fulfillment, but they must first learn tolerance and compassion.

The Sun-Moon inconjunct indicates emotive difficulties. These natives tend to be either emotionally reserved or emotionally over-wrought. The former have difficulty feeling or accepting their emotions, while the latter are prone to emotional excesses. The reserved types tend to attract controlled people who cannot tolerate emotionality or who ridicule the expression of strong feelings. This serves to discourage emotional sharing and reinforces the tendency to inhibit feeling. Sometimes the opposite may occur: the natives may become involved with people who embarrass them through emotional excess. The inability to accept their own feelings creates a need, in many natives, to justify their feelings before they can act. This leads them to quietly suffer while they build a case for their feelings. After a while, when they have enough justification, they overreact and catch people by surprise. They may then reject the person they feel so emotional about. The expression of feeling does not clear the air or open a channel for communication, but, rather, accompanies a rejection.

This aspect indicates that issues of acceptance/rejection and approval/disapproval are of primary importance. These natives can be extremely judgmental and disapproving. They also are concerned with other people's opinions. Their strong need for both acceptance and approval dominates their lives and attracts them to critical or intolerant people. They then get caught up in trying to win acceptance or approval from people who withhold or offer it conditionally. They seem drawn to those who reject or humiliate them, and attempt to force themselves into situations where they are unwanted. An extreme sensitivity to betrayal makes them oversuspicious, but, in many cases, they invite or actually set themselves up for it. They seem attracted to people who demand loyalty but who do not reciprocate. A powerful need for acceptance causes them to explain and justify themselves. They seem to be apologetic about their existence, and play roles for approval and social acceptance. They may develop a maternal, nurturing or supportive life style. They must learn to discern where this is a natural inclination and where it has the ulterior motive of winning acceptance, and then act accordingly.

This aspect indicates a struggle against social conditioning. These natives have been taught to live in fear of disapproval. They now struggle against social pressure to find meaning, purpose and direction in life. They must learn to stick to their purposes and not worry about the approval of others. They must also stop trying to prove themselves to others. Some natives become defiant and reject socially accepted roles. They engage in disapproved activities or vocations and develop a defiant life style. They say that they don't care what others think but, they really do. These people can be dominating. They take the position that their way is the only way and may express contempt for the socially accepted life style and those who live it. People with this aspect should be aware that their emotions may have a great impact on their health. They should, therefore, try to develop emotional equanimity.

This inconjunct develops an interest and concern for the feelings of others, which may be useful in the field of psychology, public relations or theater. Natives might find fulfillment in food or health-related vocations. They might also become good teachers or writers. Their discerning nature makes them good critics, but they must remember to go easy on people.

SUN INCONJUNCT MERCURY

The theme here is acceptance of new ideas. these natives are learning to speak simply, listen to others and overcome the resistance to new ideas. They are challenged to accept constructive criticism, forego self-justification and stop playing roles.

This aspect indicates a potential for expressing things in an interesting way. These natives have a talent for getting people to consider new views by motivating them to learn how to make new or unpopular ideas palatable through metaphor, allusion or humor. Their ability to draw people out permits them to help others think things through and make intelligent decisions. These natives eventually overcome early life difficulties and develop first-rate communications skills.

This inconjunct indicates difficulties in communication related to fear of rejection. These natives worry about their views being unwanted or unaccepted, and fear rejection for speaking up. They are attracted to intellectual snobs or elitists who make them feel inferior. Their attraction to people who reject new ideas makes them very cautious. They may, therefore, dissemble or withhold information in order to preclude rejection or gain acceptance. A tendency to be defensive about their intelligence creates difficulties in the mutual exchange of views. Their tendency to take criticism of ideas as a rejection can cause them to assert their views with such vehemence, that it intimidates others and precludes free discussion. These natives can be rejecting of even minor alterations of their views. They resist critical input and discourage people from offering any. Their tendency toward blunt speech usually reflects defiance. They anticipate rejection and, therefore, express their views in a take-it-or-leave-it manner. They may not, however, be aware of the effect this has on others. People tend to monitor what they say in order to avoid blunt responses. Natives may not realize that people avoid telling them the truth. Others are reluctant to ask questions when they don't understand and keep silent while the natives make erroneous statements.

This aspect indicates a tendency to justify one's views. These natives are attracted to and feel moved to express new or unusual ideas. Their defense of unpopular views creates opposition and a demand for validation. They are, therefore, constantly on the defensive and forced to justify their ideas. Anticipation of attack causes them to issue disclaimers or present their views apologetically. They learn to clown or speak self-deprecatingly in order to disarm others and forestall severe reactions. They eventually learn to present new ideas in nonthreatening ways and develop the ability to break through people's resistances.

There may be an overconcern with being misunderstood, misquoted or misrepresented. These natives may have their statements taken out of context and used against them. People tend to distort their words so that the original meaning is not conveyed. They find themselves having to justify or defend views they did not express and intentions which have been misrepresented. Refusal to share one's views doesn't help either, because it cannot prevent speculation, gossip or slander. These insidious influences are hard to combat because the natives' enemies do not confront them directly.

The inconjunct develops a concern for acceptance through communication. This can find application through advocacy of ideas, or through the use of communication skills to win acceptance for a cause, person, product or enterprise. This may find its expression in fields as diverse as public relations, law, advertising and psychology. These natives also have the potential for being excellent counsellors. The aspect also might find productive application in literary fields, which can bring much satisfaction because it indicates intellectual acceptance.

SUN INCONJUNCT VENUS

The theme here is self-affection. These natives are learning to accept pleasure, value themselves and make appropriate demands. They are challenged to stop playing roles, overcome the fear of rejection and stop trying to win others over.

This aspect indicates a pleasant, charming manner. These natives learn how to please people, and develop an ability to make the most out of packaging and appearance. Their ability to put others at ease creates a sense of acceptance and trust, which permits the sharing of important concerns.

There may be a need to overcome feelings of unlovability. These natives want to be liked by everyone but are attracted to people who withhold love or acceptance. They have difficulty expressing or accepting love and may attract people with the same problem. They may dwell in self-pity, but when love approaches, they depart. There is a tendency to lose interest in people who are available and to pursue rejecting people instead. A desire to be popular leads them to develop a charming personality or a seductive manner. If they become convinced that popularity depends upon beauty, they can obsess over their appearance. They may reinforce this concern by comparing themselves against very attractive people. They may work hard to enhance their appearance and seek to be noticed. Attention seems to reassure them that they are lovable, but it also makes them vain. Less attractive natives compare themselves to others, but feel unlovable because of their plainness. They refuse to take even minor steps to improve their appearance and want to be loved as they are. They might, eventually, realize that some effort to enhance their appearance will go a long way toward making them more desirable and attracting the love they need.

The Sun-Venus inconjunct indicates feelings of unworthiness and low self-esteem. These natives try hard to win people over, and are reluctant to make demands upon others. They feel unappreciated, yet cannot accept a compliment when it is offered. Inability to assert their needs allows people to take advantage of their good nature. Most natives tend to work for appreciation rather than for money. They are, therefore, underpaid and taken for granted. They cannot barter their services well because, on some level, they are grateful for being accepted, or even tolerated. They work hard only as long as they are unaccepted or taken for granted. Acknowledgment, or adequate pay, only seems to cause them to self-destructively sabotage their efforts or change their circumstances to find unappreciation elsewhere. Other natives swing to the opposite extreme and demand outrageous compensation for their efforts. This indicates overcompensation for feelings of unworthiness and low self-esteem.

This aspect indicates an overconcern with physical gratification. These natives tend to make acceptance or denial of pleasure into a big issue. The pleasure-rejecting types find it difficult to relax and enjoy themselves. They have to justify buying things for their own satisfaction and consistently live beneath their means. They may, sometimes, justify their life style through allegiance to a pleasure-rejecting philosophical or religious moral code which exalts asceticism as a virtue. Their inability to open up and enjoy life has social consequences because it causes others to lose interest in them. Other natives become immoderate or hedonistic, surrounding themselves with possessions and living beyond their means. Overindulgence in sensuality may be a substitute for unfulfilled lovingness.

This inconjunct indicates strong aesthetic opinions. These natives may find satisfaction in art, theater or aesthetic criticism. The ability to make attractive presentations can be turned to good use in sales. They also might find work in fashion or cosmetics to be satisfying because it fulfills their interest in appearance.

SUN INCONJUNCT MARS

The theme here is purposeful activity. These natives are learning to assert themselves, be considerate when they act and accept other people's procedures. They are challenged to overcome the fear of rejection, control aggressive impulses and forego the need to prove themselves.

This aspect indicates a self-reliant nature. These natives have a taste for individual initiative. They want to act in order to further their purposes. The desire to take initiative and ability to motivate people gives them excellent leadership potential.

This aspect indicates difficulty in the expression of aggression. Some repress their aggressive instincts while others become very aggressive. The former find it difficult to take initiative or assert themselves. They attract people who discourage assertiveness or initiative, and gravitate toward circumstances which make it impossible to take initiative. These natives tend to be passive, presenting a mild exterior or developing a bland personality. They may experience claustrophobic feelings in relationship. The more aggressive natives tend to be hard working and physically active, striving to prove themselves strong, active and courageous, or taking pains to develop physical prowess. They may have romantic feelings or heroic fantasies. There may be a fear of rejection if they back down because, to them, backing down is an admission of cowardice. They may, therefore, take foolhardy risks. They can be very susceptible to challenge because of a need to prove that they dare. The tendency to attract people who accept their strengths, but not their weaknesses, puts them under great pressure to perform. Some of these natives have low tolerance for frustration and may become violent when thwarted.

The Sun-Mars inconjunct indicates a tendency to hide or deny one's strength or power. These natives may be reluctant to assert themselves because others may think it improper. Instead, they may attempt to experience their power vicariously. These people may either subtly compete with others or be attracted to people who will act out their needs. Their aggressive needs may sometimes lead them into abusive relationships. Some of these natives may be victims of threats, battering or sexual abuse. Other natives may force themselves into forbidden roles or situations, and enter into unacceptable occupations, against the threat of social rejection. They may, in the process, suffer all sorts of attacks or privations.

This aspect indicates an excessive need for action. There is a tendency to act without consideration of the consequences. These natives, therefore, wind up acting first and apologizing later. They may attract people who force them to justify their actions. They may be unable to act unless they can explain and justify their intentions. Some if these natives can be set in their ways and resist the challenge of doing things differently. They also may attract people who resist new ways of doing things. These natives ultimately develop a philosophy about war and peace, health, hard work and right action. The need for action eventually leads them to accept risk as a fact of life.

There is leadership potential with this inconjunct. These natives are the self-starters that many businesses seek. The ability to act purposefully and take initiative makes them natural executives. They need physical activity, if not in their work, then in their recreation. Sports and exercise are good outlets for their energies. Vocations such as carpentry, plumbing, physical education, police work or the military might fulfill much of their physical needs.

SUN INCONJUNCT JUPITER

The theme here is self-assessment. These natives are learning to be generous, see themselves in perspective and develop a philosophy of life. They are challenged to overcome the fear of rejection, forego the need to impress others and stop trying to buy people with generosity.

This aspect indicates a generous, expansive but wasteful nature. These natives are ethical and highly principled, but they can be rigidly legalistic. They may be multitalented and pursue a variety of interests. They tend to be generalists rather than specialists. These natives scatter their energies in pursuit of broad overviews instead of detailed knowledge. They can be resourceful in the pursuit of new opportunities but can also be ineptly opportunistic.

There may be an excessive need to impress people, a desire to create an impressive facade. These natives want to be seen as upright, dignified and moral. They are more likely to become opinionated or intolerant, and may alienate people through pomposity or self-righteousness. They may boast, exaggerate or make promises they can't fulfill. They attempt to assist people without being asked. Overextending themselves leads to failure, but a fear of losing face makes them seek to lay the blame else-where. They may have a good sense of humor but can't take a joke when it gets too close to them. They eventually realize that the attempt to impress people just makes things more complicated and difficult. In time, these people soften the need to prove themselves and impress others.

They may even learn to laugh at their own expense.

The Sun–Jupiter inconjunct indicates problems in assessment related to a lack of perspective. These individuals tend to blow things out of proportion, exaggerating or underestimating their own importance and misjudging others as well. They tend to be optimistic about the wrong people and belittle those they should respect. They either attract people who underestimate or have impossibly high expectations for them. These types react by issuing disclaimers or by making self-deprecating remarks. They may even fail in order to defeat other people's expectations. Many of these individuals have difficulty adjusting to success – either apologizing, avoiding or flaunting it. They may attempt to apologize for their good fortune through generosity. Many of them become intensely interested in a project (or person) and then totally abandon it (him/her), swinging from enthusiasm to neglect and back again. There is either total involvement or complete disinterest. It is all or nothing until they learn to modulate their interests.

This aspect indicates difficulties in relationship. These individuals lack confidence and feel unwanted. They think that they must purchase acceptance through generosity. Their expectation of rejection leads them to pursue people who withhold acceptance. Fear or expectation of abandonment makes it hard for them to be intimate. They tend to attract people with the same problem. These natives make it hard for others to get close to them. They resist commitments because it might compromise their freedom, and avoid social opportunities in order to preclude rejection. They make others feel rejected by neglecting to follow through on relationship opportunities. They overcome these difficulties when they accept and take risks that make closeness possible.

This inconjunct indicates a late bloomer. These natives tend to grow wiser with age, and eventually develop a life philosophy around self-acceptance. An interest in knowledge and communication makes them good writers or teachers. An interest in organization may lead to success in administration or management. They also might find success in finance, accounting or law.

SUN INCONJUNCT SATURN

The theme here is responsibility to self. These natives are learning to be more mature, take themselves seriously and accept responsibility. They are challenged to overcome the fear of rejection, avoid unnecessary burdens and stop discouraging others.

This aspect indicates a conservative and traditional nature. These natives are serious, businesslike and practical. They appreciate quality, demand competence, and have little patience for ineptitude. They stick by their decisions and resist compromise.

These natives want to be accepted as mature and responsible. A tendency to play the role of parent or teacher attracts burdensome people. They tend to assume burdens for people who fail to accept responsibility. These natives are attracted to critical and discriminating people. The need for acknowledgement from authorities makes them cater to authority figures who withhold acceptance or grant it conditionally. They seem attracted to people who hesitate to accept them because of age differences or inexperience. Things don't come easily for theses natives. They have to persevere if they want to succeed. Time and resources need to be budgeted carefully if they want to accomplish things. They must learn to be economical without becoming miserly, be generous with time to people who need it and be patient with those who delay them.

The Sun-Saturn inconjunct indicates difficulty in relating due to feelings of isolation. These natives tend to feel separated from others. A sense of anxiety creates subtle defenses which keep them from accepting people uncritically. This creates barriers to closeness because others perceive them as critical, severe or impatient. Many natives feel shy or awkward in groups. Inexperience and feelings of isolation keep them from participating or competing in social situations. They tend to be observers rather than participants in life. The tendency to reach out to others from feelings of loneliness creates an oppressive aura which pushes people away. They can overcome these tendencies by developing a genuine interest in others, being less guarded and gaining social experience through participation and involvement.

This aspect indicates a tendency to be critical and pessimistic. These natives tend to measure themselves and others by very high standards. A discriminating nature makes it difficult to accept imperfection. They worry about validation and feel compelled to prove their projects. They become skeptical and employ pseudoscientific methods. An overconcern with proof and justification makes them test and retest other people's ideas before accepting them. Their critical nature turns realism into pessimism. Lack of faith keeps them from accepting new possibilities. These natives have to learn to present themselves in less restrictive or inhibitive ways, for their pessimism can discourage or defeat people.

This inconjunct indicates a sense of responsibility and pragmatism that may be exploited in business. These natives carry a natural authority, which might assist them in supervisory positions. An interest in economy might make them efficient managers. They may develop an interest in accountancy or system analysis. A skeptical or discriminating nature might attract them to law, science or engineering.

SUN INCONJUNCT URANUS

The theme here is individuality. These natives are learning to resist conformity, take a stand and tolerate the differences of others. They are challenged to overcome the fear of rejection, resist the impulse to self-justification and stop provoking people.

This aspect indicates an original and inventive nature. These natives are interested in the new and unusual. They are intellectually competitive, independent thinkers, with an ability to attain penetrating insights. There is an ability for abstract thought, but this same trait tends to make them impersonal. These natives can be very idealistic when it comes to freedom and independence. They ultimately develop a life philosophy around individuality.

The Sun-Uranus inconjunct indicates a conflict between individuality and social acceptance. These natives have a strong sense of individuality, which they feel compelled to guard. They seem attracted to people who perceive individualism as rebelliousness, and are intolerant of eccentricities. They may repress independent urges. If they conform, they do it in a quiet or subtle protest, which can take the form of eccentric or unpredictable behavior. Some natives worry about being rejected because they look or act differently. They may feel a need to justify their differences or apologize for individualistic tendencies. Some natives want to break with the past, but can't do this openly, while other natives defiantly adopt radical views. The challenge here is to find the middle ground between giving society what it needs without sacrificing one's individuality.

These natives want to be original and creative. They want to do things their own way, but lack the discipline to achieve things by themselves. They are either attracted to rebellious people who withhold complete acceptance, or conservative people who resist their creative endeavors. They tend to hide strong feelings behind a mild exterior. Many natives have difficulty expressing anger directly and experience tension or anxiety. Perverseness, erraticness or inconsistency become subtle ways of striking back. Some natives desire to shock by playing devil's advocate. The tendency to attack others' basic premises at a root level makes people fear or resent them. They want to upset structures but leave nothing to fill the void. The need to shock people into realization merely creates resistance. They would be better off learning to use humor or allegory to get the message across.

There may be a resistance to close relationship due to an excessive need for independence. These natives may avoid close involvement because they fear compromise of personal freedom or independence. They tend toward impersonality and often prefer friendship, or arm's length intimacy, to marriage. They may attract impersonal people who keep them at a distance. They can be willfully set in their ways and intolerant of other people's habits or eccentricities. Their own unusual habits discourage others from living with them as well. These natives may be reluctant to trust people because they fear sudden rejection or reversals of fortune. They attract people who confirm this fear and reinforce the need to remain separate.

This inconjunct indicates a natural inclination toward original and independent effort. These natives might be drawn to writing, art or other creative activities. An original approach to problems might indicate a talent for trouble shooting or invention. A rebellious and independent mind might point to legal talent. They might make good lawyers, advocates or shop stewards.

SUN INCONJUNCT NEPTUNE

The theme here is acceptance of obligation. These natives are learning to use imagination, make commitments and accept the spiritual dimensions of life. They are challenged to overcome the fear of rejection, communicate clearly and avoid escapist tendencies.

This aspect indicates a highly imaginative nature. These natives have a taste for art, music or poetry. An ability to visualize permits them to use imagination effectively. Mystical tendencies and religious inclinations lead to the development of strong spiritual values. They ultimately learn to integrate mystical sensibilities into a coherent life philosophy and inspire others to faith.

The Sun-Neptune inconjunct indicates difficulties in making and sticking to decisions. These natives tend to be indecisive. Suggestibility and impractical goals make it difficult for them to make realistic decisions. The tendency to operate from confused or ambivalent motives causes vacillation. Decisions based upon idealistic considerations require frequent revision. Aimlessness and lack of clarity serve to undermine their authority. A major part of the problem is a tendency to conform to the needs of others and accept unfair obligations. People, therefore, tend to take them for granted and presume to make further demands. These natives tend to be too easily affected by other people's feelings. An unwillingness to disappoint others causes them to apologize for their actions and justify their intentions. A desire for acceptance makes it difficult to implement the decisions they do make and undermines their effectiveness. These natives become more forceful when they realize that indecision does not win acceptance, but, rather, contempt for weakness.

There may be difficulty in daily life due to escapist tendencies. These natives may have a rich fantasy life. Over-imaginative inclinations and romantic notions make it difficult for them to see things as they really are. Fantasy and indulgence in daydream impedes productivity and undermines effectiveness. Absentmindedness causes costly errors. Many natives try to conform to popular social models. The tendency to relate to others from illusion results in disappointment. Drugs or alcohol may, sometimes, provide escape routes from the commitments and pressures of daily life. These natives must take care not to overindulge themselves, for they may, in time, become sensitized to stimulants.

This aspect indcates problems due to ambivalence and self-doubt. These natives find it difficult to accept themselves. Self-doubt and inner uncertainty causes them to seek reassurance from others. Lack of faith in their projects makes them supersensitive to criticism. They, therefore, they feel compelled to explain or justify themselves. Many natives attract people who show a false interest in them, withhold acceptance or else extend it conditionally. There is a strong tendency to make commitments or take on obligations in order to win acceptance. Uncertainty of purpose or intention creates confusion in communication. Conflicting signals, double meanings and mixed messages make mutual understanding impossible. These natives experience ambivalence from others until they clarify their own motives. They must forego the temptation to harbor illusions about others and accept people as they are in order to find fulfillment in relationship.

This inconjunct indicates a potential talent for visual or imagistic activities such as art, photography or film. An attraction to illusion might suggest theater, fashion or cosmetology as potential occupations. Mystical inclinations might point the way to poetry, music or religion. These natives also might find employment as drug counselors or, perhaps, bartenders.

SUN INCONJUNCT PLUTO

The theme here is acceptance of change. These natives are learning to tolerate uncertainty, be diplomatic and accept other people's beliefs. They are challenged to put aside obsessions, overcome the fear of rejection and be less dogmatic.

This aspect indicates a persistent nature, with an ability to investigate, analyze and plan. These natives have a psychological bent. They want to know what makes people tick. They may be motivated by a desire to reform or transform others, but they must learn to temper penetrating insights with tact and diplomacy. Perseverance is one of their major assets, but they must also let go of old intentions in order to permit self-renewal.

The Sun-Pluto inconjunct indicates difficulty in relationship due to a need for control and certainty. These natives can become obsessed with a fear of rejection and may develop a "what if" attitude, which makes them constantly worry about the future. The need to be absolutely certain of other people's feelings makes them sensitive to the slightest nuances in other's reactions. A tendency to assume the worst makes them clinging and oppressive. Fear of uncertainty makes them interrogate people about their feelings or intentions. Fear of the unexpected and a need to anticipate all possibilities makes them obsess about the future. They want to know what to expect so that they can be prepared for it. Their need to know the details of people's lives leaves others with too little privacy and finally pushes them away. Many natives attract obsessive or clinging people. They also seem attracted to manipulative people who control them by withholding acceptance or threatening rejection.

There may be a tendency toward obsessive behavior. These natives seem to obsess about everything in their lives. They may worry about work, health, hygiene or personal appearance. Some of these natives are obsessively neat, while others are slovenly. The former cannot tolerate disorder and seem repelled by disarray. Many natives have difficulty living in the present. They either fantasize about the future or think about the past. They may feel apologetic about their own existence. Apology, justification and explanation are constant concerns. Wherever they are, whatever they do, they want to be ready to explain or justify themselves. Their excuses or explanations are carefully thought out and rehearsed. They tend to analyze, analyze, analyze and think out, figure out, work out the reasons, meanings, intentions, motivations and analyze, analyze still further. They want to know exactly what they are doing and why they are doing it in order to explain themselves to others. They have a compulsion to verify and prove. Real life, however, cannot be so thoroughly anticipated, and these natives wind up having to scotch their carefully prepared arguments. They tend to be stilted and unspontaneous, clinging to agendas which are patently inappropriate because of an intolerance for uncertainty. These natives also may be very doctrinaire or dogmatic. They resist change and try to ignore the things that don't conform to their preconceived notions. They eventually come to realize that they cannot pigeonhole life, and learn to relax and develop a be-here-now philosophy. They learn to accept change and let go of their obsessions.

This inconjunct indicates potential talent for healing. These natives might make excellent psychologists or medical doctors. They may find satisfaction in research and analysis. An interest and ability to transform others' feelings may interest them in sales, advertising or theater.

SUN INCONJUNCT ASC/DSC

The theme here is tolerance. Theses natives are learning to cooperate with others, develop relationships and accept people as they are. They are challenged to stop complaining, overcome the fear of rejection and resist the impulse to self-justification.

This aspect indicates a potential for developing a charismatic personality. These natives possess natural leadership ability. They inspire people through strong character, clear intention and sense of purpose. They can be persevering in creative activity. Health and physical well-being become progressively more important to them as they grow older. They eventually develop a philosophy of life which emphasizes the need for physical activity.

This inconjunct points to acceptance/rejection as the central issue in one's life. These natives have a strong urge to win acceptance or overcome rejection. An inferiority complex makes them defensive about themselves or their projects. They may become apologetic or self-justifying. Need for attention either makes them shy or forces them to develop a strong personality. They may court people, hide behind roles or try to make themselves needed. Some of these natives try to force themselves into unwanted situations, trying to overcome unacceptance or rejection. Most natives try to avoid the possibility of rejection. They are, however, attracted to people who give conditional acceptance. They must find their inner direction and stick to their purposes, because the need for acceptance permits other people to pull them away from their centers. They must be careful, however, to avoid becoming rejecting or intolerant themselves.

The Sun-ASC/DSC inconjunct indicates problems in relationship due to unwillingness to compromise. These natives can't seem to accept people as they are. They avoid close relationships or seek involvement with rejecting people. They may use people as screens for their projections. There is a tendency to seek vicarious fulfillment through partners. These natives feel forced to deny themselves in order to save relationships, but they resist compromise with partners. They can be cranky or discontented, or may attract people who love to complain. Quarrels about money or children create division. They can either be indecisive or rigid and uncompromising. Once they make a decision they stick to it. When they decide to reject someone, they don't give them another chance.

There is a need to find fulfillment through meaningful work. It is, therefore, extremely important for these natives to find suitable vocations. Until they find their work, they feel their lives to be aimless, purposeless or meaningless. They can't seem to find real satisfaction in relationship, avocation or amusement, as other people do. To them work is the essential ingredient which gives life meaning and brings satisfaction. They eventually develop a philosophy of life around work, health and relationship. They ultimately may come to lead an integrated life, in which what one does is not different from what one is.

This inconjunct permits one to use personality very effectively. These natives may develop an ability to engage others and to play roles. It is a good aspect for an actor or salesman. Interest in health might lead them to become doctors, physical therapists, psychologists, dieticians, etc. A critical nature might lead to critical writing. Ability to interact with others in a contentious environment can lead them to become marriage counselors, mediators or negotiators.

SUN INCONJUNCT MC/IC

The theme here is acceptance of authority. These natives are learning to accept social status, play leadership roles and develop a social philosophy. They are challenged to overcome the fear of rejection, put aside resentment and stop trying to overshadow others.

This aspect indicates a social conscience. These natives have feelings of compassion for the downtrodden and a need to confront society with the urgency for change. They develop the ability to influence society to consider new directions. They also have personal power and leadership ability, but they must learn to use their powers for the larger good.

This aspect indicates a need to prove oneself through career. These natives feel a need to make authorities accept them. They seem, however, attracted to negative and rejecting authority figures who make them explain or justify themselves or their projects. They tend to identify with important figures of the past, and play the role of parent or authority figure to others. Many of these natives seek to develop personal power through profession. Career, therefore, becomes very important to them, and they may easily identify with their career or professional function. Some natives seek to enter careers or professions which exclude them, and they may be forced to deal with colleagues who make them feel unwelcome. Many natives feel forced to choose between career advancement and family life. They can't seem to accept that sacrifice of one for the other is required, and make themselves miserable longing for the thing they voluntarily gave up. Many natives secretly desire power, prestige or influence (they might deny this, even to themselves) but don't know how to use power when they get it. The tendency to be excessively cautious or petty in the application of power irritates others and engenders frustration. They can, if they aren't careful, finally get people to rebel against and openly oppose their authority.

The Sun-MC/IC inconjunct indicates a tendency to rebel against established authority. These natives live with frustration, resentment and anxiety. They seem to be dominated by an internalized resentful child who finds it hard to be playful. A fear of society may lead them to reject society. They can't seem to accept the world as it is and want society to accede to their wishes. Although critical and rebellious, they tend to back down when challenged. They want to be purposeful, but also want permission to act. Some natives find it difficult to tolerate opposition. They may become resentful or vindictive when thwarted. They might, alternatively, have to deal with people who become vengeful when frustrated. These natives are natural social rebels who want to confront the world with the need for change and find meaning in life by championing the oppressed. They challenge the established order, and, therefore, incur the wrath of conservative authorities. Their objections to tradition are often well-founded. They, therefore, fulfill the useful social function of confronting the established system with the need for review and modification of its policies.

This inconjunct conveys personal power and leadership ability. These natives may make good business executives, administrators or teachers. An ability to make charismatic and potent presentations may be helpful in sales, theater or artistic endeavors. These natives also might find success in writing or in advocacy professions, such as law. They also may make good doctors or healers.

MOON INCONJUNCT MERCURY

The theme here is conditioned thought v. honesty of expression. These natives are learning to think independently, be less judgmental and stand up to social pressure. They are challenged to forego the need for approval and accept constructive criticism.

This aspect tends to make one very perceptive, perhaps psychic. It confers an ability to move people through emotional appeal. These natives tend to become effective at written and verbal communication. They learn to break down the barriers to communication and understanding when they lose their shyness and fear of critical judgment. They begin to communicate simply and naturally and become skilled at getting others to review emotionally based views.

There may be a concern about one's mental prowess or communication skills. These natives often find it difficult to assess the impact of their words upon others. The anticipation of being misunderstood or misrepresented may lead them to withhold their views from others. The need for approval or the desire to avoid disapproval may lead them to purposely dissemble. Some natives may tell lies in order to avoid embarrassment. Other natives avoid speaking up or asking questions because they fear making fools of themselves by revealing their ignorance. Some natives are attracted to unpopular views, which they express adamantly. They tend to be blunt with people who question or doubt their ideas, and thin-skinned when their views are criticized. They can feel betrayed by friends who offer constructive criticism. Betrayal, in general, seems to be a very important concern for these natives. They worry about being betrayed or embarrassed by gossip or indiscretion and make it a point to demonstrate their loyalty though verbal support. These concerns sometimes come to pass because there is a tendency to attract people who will betray them.

The Moon–Mercury inconjunct indicates a tendency to be judgmental. These natives tend to sit in judgment of other people's ideas, approving or disapproving, either silently or vocally. They also tend to attract critical and judgmental people who deny or withhold approval. Some natives seem to attract verbal abuse or humiliation. It would be profitable for them to put aside excessive judgment of ideas and accept people less critically. This will then attract the same treatment from others.

This aspect indicates difficulty in emotional expression. These natives either hide their feelings behind a screen of rationality or are excessively emotional. The former find it difficult to be spontaneous with their feelings. In some cases, the aspect indicates a tendency to be out of touch with one's feelings. The latter types may become so emotionally overwrought that they have difficulty thinking rationally. Here, feeling overwhelms thought or perception. These natives are faced with the challenge of finding the right balance between the rational and the emotional. Once this is achieved, they learn how to express their feelings effectively and can imbue words with great emotive power.

This inconjunct develops an ability to convey feeling forcefully through words. These natives may find both satisfaction and success in acting, writing or humor. Publishing, advertising, public relations or teaching also may be fruitful areas of endeavor.

MOON INCONJUNCT VENUS

The theme here is self-approval. These natives are rediscovering their worth, learning to make demands and coming to understand the relative importance of appearance. They are challenged to stop seeking approval and trying to win others over.

This aspect tends to indicate strong aesthetic sensibilities and severe tastes. These natives can be very opinionated when it comes to art or creative endeavors. There is a knack for intuiting what the public will respond to. They tend to be very good in social situations, know how to put people at ease, and make them feel comfortable.

This inconjunct may create a concern with being liked by everyone. These natives may so fear displeasing others that they become reluctant to express their true feelings. They may, therefore, express only superficial pleasantries. Some natives make themselves popular by developing a pleasing appearance and demeanor. Popularity seems to reassure them that they are 100% lovable, but they can become vain and superficial. Other natives use their social awkwardness to reinforce their feelings of un-lovability. Many of these people feel inferior because of an unattractive appearance but refuse to do anything to improve themselves. They seem to be saying "love me as I am." What they are actually saying is: "Give me satisfaction even though I offer you none in return." Sooner or later, they come to realize that other people will become interested in them as soon as they make themselves more interesting or attractive. They can, however, be judgmental of other people's appearance. Minor imperfections so put them off that they may find it difficult to enjoy the company of others.

The Moon-Venus inconjunct often indicates low self-esteem. These natives tend to believe that love and approval must be earned from moment to moment. Feelings of intrinsic unlovability attract them to people who withhold love or appreciation. They run from love toward disapproval and humiliation. Their inability to accept love reflects an inability to give love. A tendency to feel more comfortable with humiliation than love attracts them to masochistic involvements. Many of these natives seem attracted to flirtatious or fickle partners who threaten them with betrayal. Some natives actually encourage or set themselves up for betrayal, and then feel sorry for themselves when it happens. This tends to reinforce feelings of unworthiness and unlovability. Most of these people work hard for approval but find it difficult to accept appreciation when it is offered. They also have difficulty demanding appropriate rewards for their efforts. Some work for meager pay in the hope for appreciation or approval, while other natives make exorbitant demands or charge excessive fees. Some may even betray others for money, property or possessions.

This inconjunct indicates talent in art, music and other creative endeavors. These natives may find vocational success in theater, commercial art, fashion, cosmetics. The interest in relaxing people or making them comfortable may help attract them to public relations.

MOON INCONJUNCT MARS

The theme here is finding the right balance between consideration for others and the need for action. These natives are learning to stand up to social conditioning and assert themselves in an appropriate manner. They are challenged to give up the need to prove themselves, forego the temptation to judge others and stop worrying about other people's opinions.

This aspect indicates strong feelings. These natives have plenty of passion and a strong romantic nature. Their emotional responses are quick and sharp, and they tend to stick to their guns when they think they are right. These people tend to be independent and have plenty of initiative. They can be the self-starters that business is always seeking. They develop original procedures and stand up to people who disapprove of their methods. An ability to act with fidelity inspires and motivates others.

There may be difficulty in expressing strong emotion. These natives are either emotionally inhibited or excessive. The former can't seem to express anger appropriately and consequently feel frustrated or fearful. They may even be immobilized by strong feelings, such as fear or anger. They may avoid asserting themselves because they fear disapproval or retaliation, and may hide their feelings in order to avoid provoking others. They can be outwardly stoic while suffering inner turmoil. Because of this, they may suffer from assorted aches and pains, depression, ulcers or intestinal disorders. The latter, more emotional types also have difficulty handling anger. Their problem is lack of self-restraint. These natives tend to have short fuses and hot tempers. They react too quickly and then regret it. The former types tend to live in fear of violence but, ironically, seem drawn to abusive relationships. The latter types are more likely to be the abusers than the victims. These natives are attracted to their opposite types until they learn to express their feelings appropriately.

The Moon–Mars inconjunct indicates a desire to win approval through physical activity. These natives tend to have an emotional investment in their work. They put their hearts into it because it may, perhaps, be a way of sublimating their feelings. This means that emotions either stimulate or preclude activity. A need to win approval for their efforts sometimes allows others to take advantage of them. They work hard for acknowledgment, but leave themselves open to manipulation by people who withhold approval. These natives have original approaches to problems, but are frustrated by the need for approval before they act. They may work for people who criticize their efforts continually. They free themselves when they stop worrying about other people's opinions and act on their own inner needs.

This aspect can create a need to develop and display strength and courage. These natives tend to feel humiliated by weakness or cowardice. Their strongly romantic nature prizes freedom, self-reliance and heroism. The need to overcome or deny their fears causes them to, foolishly, accept all challenges. Many of these natives have strong sexual drives which they strive to control. Their perception of betrayal as humiliation makes them become infuriated when they feel betrayed, but they often invite it. Some natives develop defiant life styles which oppose social conventions. They can be violent and promiscuous, but they can also apply double standards of conventionality to partners.

This inconjunct indicates leadership ability. These natives have an ability to act quickly and directly. They can inspire and motivate others through example. They may make good project leaders or business executives. High energy levels might suit these natives for physical vocations such as carpentry, plumbing or other manual work. They also might find fulfillment and physical release through dance, sports or physical exercise.

MOON INCONJUNCT JUPITER

The major theme here is development of compassion. These natives are learning to be milder in their judgments, assess people accurately and open themselves to intimate relationships. They are challenged to stop trying to impress people or buy them with generosity.

This aspect indicates an encouraging, expansive, generous nature. These natives can be compassionate, supportive and loyal. An openness to emotional appeal allows them to be influenced by other people's feelings. A strong moral code makes them trustworthy and ethical. Attainment of emotional perspective permits them to council others and help people manage their affairs. A good heart and a beneficent nature may, however, attract emotionally needy people.

There may be difficulty in emotional expression. These natives find it hard to express feelings appropriately. They either keep strong feelings hidden behind an optimistic facade or indulge in emotional excesses. The first type may restrain feelings because they feel it undignified or humiliating to express themselves openly. These natives may involve themselves with overly emotional people who embarrass them through excess. Alternately, they may be involved with repressed people who belittle open displays of feeling. The second type can't seem to keep emotions under control and feel humiliated after they vent feelings inappropriately. They tend to undermine themselves and lose opportunities through emotional excess. Both types eventually learn when to control or use feelings for effect and when to simply vent for release.

The Moon-Jupiter inconjunct indicates an excessive need to win approval. The need to impress others may sometimes lead them to exaggerate. They are likely to be generous and giving to people who do not reciprocate. The tendency to be attracted to judgmental people who disapprove or belittle them prevents them from finding fulfillment. Lack of faith in their own abilities or resources keeps them from taking advantage of available opportunities. Expectation of failure and fear of humiliation keeps them from taking the risks which might lead to success. These natives also tend to be highly judgmental of others as well. A tendency to criticize and disapprove leads them to unintentionally withhold approval and attracts the same treatment from others. They stop worrying about what others think when they forego the temptation to sit in judgment of others. This type eventually learns to encourage people by expressing approval and optimism.

This aspect indicates difficulty in relationship due to poor judgment.

These natives tend to misjudge people badly. They trust the wrong people and seem attracted to those who will belittle, humiliate or betray them. They tend to wrongly assess the talents or abilities of others, and can be too easily impressed by facades. They try hard to live up to people's expectations. Many of these natives find it difficult to get close to others. They may involve themselves with fickle or inconstant people. Their tendency to worry about abandonment or the possibility of betrayal may lead them, unconsciously, to invite or set themselves up for such situations. These difficulties are overcome when they develop faith in their intuitions and learn to trust their feelings. With age, they become progressively wiser in the art of relationship.

This inconjunct permits the use of feeling in the literary or communication fields. These natives can learn to use emotional appeal to create new opportunities. They may be successful at advertising, sales or promotion. An ability to encourage or reassure people helps them instill confidence in others. They can help others to expand their horizons by encouraging them to take the risks that growth demands. They, therefore, may make good counselors. An ability to manage affairs helps them to succeed in administrative or managerial situations. These natives also might make good teachers.

MOON INCONJUNCT SATURN

The theme here is the development of emotional maturity. These natives are learning to accept responsibility, respect other people's feelings and stand up to oppressive tradition. They are challenged to be less judgmental, stop worrying about what others think and take social risks.

This aspect indicates a strong sense of responsibility. These natives tend to be sensitive and discriminating, economical and realistic. They have the discipline and strength of character to function under hardship and adversity. The general demeanor is sober and they find it difficult to be lighthearted. They have good control over their feelings, but they must learn to be more comfortable with emotional expression.

This inconjunct indicates difficulty in emotional expression due to a need to be seen as mature. These natives want to be recognized as mature and responsible. The tendency to equate emotionality with immaturity makes them try to control their feelings. They try to hide their emotions behind a serious demeanor. When they do express themselves, there is a tendency to reveal their feelings to critical or disapproving people. They may feel forced to wait interminably before they can show their feelings. They wind up expressing emotions at inappropriate times, usually too late. They can be cautious or defensive, rather than open. Self-protection inhibits openness and responsiveness. Self-alienation keeps them out of touch with their own feelings or makes them doubt what they feel. They can be very self-critical over the feelings they do have. They try to present a stoic facade but, inwardly, they suffer from feelings of inferiority or melancholy. Fear of emotional breakdown or loss of control makes it difficult for them to cry. These natives have to be careful, for in their need to show maturity and control, they also tend to invite parental projections from others. They may, therefore, attract emotionally immature people who lean on them for support.

There may be a tendency to accept burdens and responsibilities in order to win approval. These natives tend to seek respect from critical or disapproving authority figures. They tend to be attracted to people who withhold approval unless they meet impossibly high standards. They feel forced to be responsible both for themselves and others and can wind up being taken for granted. Punctuality is very important for these natives and they hate to be kept waiting. However, they may sometimes embarrass themselves through tardiness. Many of these natives try to live up to impossibly high standards of perfection. Their judgmental and critical nature tempts them to look upon people disparagingly. They tend to see others as irresponsible and immature and themselves as realistic and responsible. A pessimistic attitude takes the fun out of life. If these natives learn to lighten up and laugh, they can help others become more realistic without inhibiting the joy in living.

The Moon-Saturn inconjunct indicates difficulty in relationship due to feelings of separateness. These natives often feel lonely and isolated. They can't seem to reach out to others emotionally, and set up barriers to feeling and relating. They find it difficult to compete in social situations and tend to feel awkward in groups. The tendency to feel more comfortable as observer than participant keeps them out of social activities. Some natives dwell upon the past instead of initiating new social contacts. They may not take the time to develop relationships. They can be very loyal friends, but worry about the possibility of betrayal. Fear of betrayal makes them suspicious, inhibits trust and precludes real closeness. Overconcern with betrayal inevitably invites or creates it. They can overcome this tendency when they put aside their fears and learn to trust their instincts.

This inconjunct may find fruitful release where sensitivity, discipline and controlled emotional expression are important. This may be useful in mastering a musical instrument. The ability to be rational and realistic in spite of feelings gives these natives leadership potential. They can be excellent teachers, if they will only lighten their critical and pessimistic manner. They can become good judges of character. The ability to master the art of timing in human affairs might endow them with a gift for business management.

MOON INCONJUNCT URANUS

The theme here is the conflict between conformity and individuality. These natives are learning to break with social conditioning and accept disapproval as the price for emotional freedom. They are challenged to moderate their provocative nature and be less defiant.

This aspect tends to indicate quickness and unpredictability of emotional responses. These natives have finely tuned nervous systems in which feeling and intuition combine to create a powerful sixth sense. They have a knack for creating excitement. They arouse others, and create tension and anxiety. Their feelings trigger new ideas. They are nonconformist and iconoclastic and very original in their shocking manner.

The Moon-Uranus inconjunct tends to indicate an anxious need to avoid disapproval. These natives seem to attract judgmental people who disapprove of originality and independence. They may be seen as eccentric or perverse and derided for their differences. They tend to be caught in the bind of wanting to rebel against the very people from whom they seek approval. Many natives develop judgmental or disapproving attitudes. They become either creative originals who disparage the creativity of others or the conservatives who disapprove of reform. Natives who conform and live conventional lives often find themselves having to contend with their rebellious counterparts. This lends support to the adage: Either you do it yourself, or you attract people who act it out for or upon you.

Natives with this aspect may be emotionally guarded because they anticipate sudden betrayal. They either attract rational, repressed people who cannot tolerate excitement and anger, or irrational excitable types who cannot restrain themselves. In either case, they are forced to hide their feelings behind a calm facade. They may be mental and impersonal rather than vital and intimate. Some natives find release for their strong feelings through perversity or eccentricity, while other types develop passive aggressive tendencies. The former enjoy shocking or upsetting people by their actions or attitudes, while the latter irritate people through lateness, inconsistency or unreliability. Some natives develop a defiant attitude toward society. They do as they please in spite of social disapproval, and lead independent, nonconformist life styles. In the end, they develop a contemptuous attitude toward social conventions and deride those who live by society's rules.

This inconjunct indicates an ability to explore the roots of the past. It can be helpful for a researcher or writer. These natives might find success in counseling professions such as astrology or psychology. The ability to stimulate people and create effects that attract attention, which can be useful in theater, publicity or advertising.

MOON INCONJUNCT NEPTUNE

The theme here is emotional ambivalence. These natives are learning to communicate clearly and make emotional commitments. They are challenged to forego the need for approval, overcome self-doubt and avoid escapist tendencies.

This aspect indicates visual, imagistic, creative talent. These natives can be empathic and impressionable, perhaps psychic. They are attracted to musical, artistic or poetic expression and may have a talent for expressing other people's feelings, fantasies or illusions. A rich fantasy life may, at times, lead them to confuse illusion with reality.

This inconjunct indicates a tendency to suffer from a wavering self-image. These natives may be beset with self-doubt and tend to seek positive feedback from others. They attract people who prey upon this need by withholding approval or offering it conditionally. This type tends to be confused by ambivalence and double messages. Consequently, they may attract people who are vacillating and ambivalent in their feelings. Some natives have difficulty assessing their impact upon others. Lack of trust in their own feelings makes them doubt their own emotional perceptions. Some types have poor memories or find it difficult to concentrate. Inattention is usually the result of escapist fantasy which removes them from the present moment. These fantasies sometimes involve thoughts or fears of humiliation. Some natives may seek escape through drugs or alcohol, while others are motivated to help people overcome this problem.

There may be difficulty in emotional expression due to uncertainty and confusion. These natives often don't know what they really feel. The tendency to pick up and express other people's emotions may create relationship problems because others react adversely when confronted by their own very secret feelings. These natives may feel sad but feel pressured to feign more positive feelings. Some find themselves obligated to control their emotions, while others can't seem to develop emotional self-control. The latter type may cry excessively in order to gain sympathy. Ephemeral feelings may present a problem for these natives. They have to be careful, for their sympathetic nature may leave them open to victimization by people who feign feelings for advantage. They must, therefore, take care to avoid making commitments on the basis of transient emotions.

The Moon–Neptune inconjunct indicates that fulfillment of obligation is a sensitive issue. Acceptance of obligation becomes a trap for these natives because they can't seem to say NO! They feel pressured to accept burdens in order to avoid disapproval and consequently attract people who lean on them for emotional support. They can be loyal and ethical, but this is not reciprocated. These natives fulfill their commitments toward others but they can't seem to get people to make or fulfill commitments toward them. People tend to relate to them for ulterior motives and lose interest when their purposes are fulfilled. Many natives become very sensitive to possibilities of betrayal. They become suspicious, worry about deception and begin to distrust others. Misinterpreted statements and unintended actions become the basis for emotional overreactions. These natives eventually solve their problems when they clarify their own needs, learn to communicate more clearly and risk adverse reactions by saying no.

This inconjunct can be useful in the theater, arts or advertising. It also might be useful for artists, photographers, musicians, fund raisers, travel agents, airline attendants or bartenders. This aspect often lends itself to mystical or spiritual pursuits such as poetry or religion. These natives might be able to inspire others through visions or image-making talents.

MOON INCONJUNCT PLUTO

The theme here is emotional rigidity and the problems it causes. These natives are learning to trust others, let go of obsessive emotions and express feelings appropriately. They are challenged to be less judgmental and accept uncertainty as a way of life.

This aspect indicates psychic sensitivity and perceptiveness. These natives have a good sixth sense. The ability to pick up other people's feelings on a gut level allows them to understand people's deeper reactions and help them to change. These natives also have an instinctive feeling for group psychology. An ability to analyze and understand public reactions gives them a distinct advantage which might be used commercially or politically.

Many of these natives tend to lack emotional spontaneity. They either hide feelings behind a controlled demeanor or become fixated in one predominant emotion. The former type develops an emotional stiltedness which makes it difficult to react naturally and discourages others from developing emotional ties. They may resist showing feeling because they don't know how others will react. The latter type tends to show one constant emotion (e.g., constant fear or constant anger). These natives can be emotionally manipulative, and may learn, sooner or later, to use their powerful feelings to control others or bully them into emotional submission. They learn to use emotion for power purposes but pay the price of sacrificing emotional sharing in relationship. Most natives seem to have problems with obsessive feelings. The tendency to hang onto old memories and indulge old feelings leaves no room for the integration of new experiences. They must ultimately learn to let go of old emotions if they want to avoid becoming emotionally stagnant. If they can do this they can learn to live in the present moment.

The Moon-Pluto inconjunct often indicates obsession with winning approval or avoiding disapproval. These natives can manipulate people or be manipulated by those who withhold approval or grant it conditionally. They can be critical or judgmental, but they also attract judgmental types. They can be willful or defiant, or may have to live or deal with willful or defiant people. These natives often have agendas by which they try to live. This makes it important for them to know in advance what to expect, so that they can prepare themselves to react appropriately. Predetermined attitudes cause them to lose the ability to assess other people's emotional reactions accurately, and tends to make them very dogmatic. Attempts to manage events are usually doomed to failure because life circumstances rarely develop as anticipated. They eventually have to drop their carefully prepared agendas and learn to be more flexible.

There may be an overconcern with loyalty. These natives are very sensitive to the possibility of betrayal and develop a suspicious manner which seeks it where it doesn't even exist. The intensity of this concern tends to create betrayal scenes which are punctuated with emotional explosions. These natives are especially prone to confide in people who inadvertently embarrass them through indiscretion. Fear of uncertainty makes these natives question friends or partners to uncover hidden feelings or motivation. This obsessiveness actually winds up oppressing people and drives them away. A need for guarantees may thus, actually, create the very situations they fear.

This inconjunct indicates a talent for manipulating feeling, which might find useful expression in theater or advertising. These natives have an instinctive feeling for psychology, making them excellent psychologists or salesmen. They have the potential to motivate others through emotional appeal.

MOON INCONJUNCT ASC/DSC

The theme here is self-disapproval and fear of humiliation. These natives are learning to perceive people more clearly, express feelings appropriately and risk relationship.

The Moon-ASC/DSC inconjunct indicates compassion, emotional sensitivity and instinctive awareness. These natives are emotional tuning forks but they may not trust their feelings. Their emotional vulnerability can lead them to turn away from others and dwell upon their own inner concerns. As a result, they may lose emotional contact with people and find it hard to participate in the emotional give and take of life. They may also find it difficult to accept feedback or assess other people's feelings. This can lead them to project feelings onto others or live vicariously through the people in their lives.

This aspect indicates a tendency to have difficulty with emotional expression. These natives may be either bland and inexpressive or over-emotional. They may be forced by circumstances to inhibit or reconsider feelings, but when feeling is expressed, it can be excessive or redundant. These people tend to be attracted to either emotionally repressed or extremely emotional partners. They may, therefore, be reluctant to express feelings because it might endanger the relationship. Fear of humiliation can make these natives very shy. They try to avoid embarrassing situations but seem to be drawn to them as well. Difficulties in expressiveness and fear of embarrassment may create sexual problems. This can be overcome with the development of a genuine emotional life.

Many of these natives can be very judgmental. They can be their own worst critics, disapproving of their appearance, personal style or manner. The need to seek approval might attract judgmental people. The natives either are cranky and complaining or attract malcontented people. Some react to the concern for approval by becoming defiant or by living a defiant life style. In moderation, this can be a virtue. It permits the person to be an individual and stand up to social pressure to conform. This aspect is more likely, however, to indicate defiance as a reaction against expected social disapproval.

The Moon–ASC/DSC inconjunct indicates a great sensitivity to betrayal which sometimes leads these natives to invite it. They may try to prove their loyalty to others, but can embarrass themselves and others through indiscretion. These people may be easily swayed by momentary emotions, which can lead them to be flirtatious or fickle. They might also attract such people. These natives may be either promiscuous or sexually cautious. Either of these behaviors can result from an overconcern with the pressures of loyalty v. betrayal or the fear of humiliation.

This inconjunct helps one develop an ability to elicit feelings from people. As a consequence, one might learn to help others express their feelings. This can, therefore, be an excellent aspect for a psychologist or marriage counselor. This aspect also helps in the development of the ability to affect people through emotional appeal. It gives talent in creative or expressive pursuits such as art, music or theater. These natives have an ability for professions where sensitivity to public response is important. This might lead to success in advertising or literary fields.

MOON INCONJUNCT MC/IC

The theme here is emotional openness and honesty in the face of social pressure. These natives are learning to express their feelings, stand up to disapproval and be more socially aware. They are challenged to overcome resentment, be less defiant and avoid emotional tyranny.

This aspect indicates sensitivity and psychic attunement, especially in regard to the public. This means that these natives have a good ability to deal with people and a knack for anticipating public trends. Their empathy and sensitivity gives them the potential of giving voice to unexpressed public resentments. These people also develop an awareness of how those in authority feel. This gives the potential of dealing with public issues by bringing conflicting sides together. However, this is often done at the expense of the native's own feelings, which must be held in abeyance.

The Moon-MC/IC inconjunct indicates problems with emotional expression. These natives may find themselves having to hold back feelings because of social position and responsibility, or in deference to parents, family or superiors. There may be pressure to make concessions to family or superiors. Many of these natives suffer from feelings of frustration or resentment. They would really love to throw a tantrum but would be too embarrassed to do so. They want permission to express their feelings, but resent having to ask for it. These natives may be attracted to work situations which require emotional control. They may guard their feelings intentionally for political reasons or in order to further their careers.

There is usually a tendency to either seek approval or avoid disapproval from parents, superiors or authority figures. These natives may be put in the position of proving their loyalty to family or superiors who then disappoint or betray them. Many of these people have strong internal judges who disapprove of everything and everyone. They also seem to attract themselves to disapproving superiors whom they try to win over. There is a tendency to walk through life judging everyone and worrying about being judged as well. Their belief that the world disapproves of them may lead them to become defiant or live defiant life styles. These natives may become disapproving authority figures or petty tyrants once they are given some power. They can be suspicious and demanding. A judgmental and humiliating nature may alienate superiors as well as subordinates. They may actually encourage the very betrayal situations they fear.

This inconjunct is useful for working with people. These natives might make good salesmen, psychologists, writers or actors. They also might be good buyers or public relations people. Fulfillment may be found in union work, where they can express grievances for others and defy authorities. The ability to bring others together also might make these people good mediators.

MERCURY INCONJUNCT VENUS

The theme her is truth v. euphemism. These natives are learning to value their own ideas, accept criticism and become more diplomatic. They are challenged to communicate more directly and stop trying to win others over.

The Mercury-Venus inconjunct indicates a talent for putting people at ease. These natives can be considerate and tactful. They develop a pleasant manner and an ability to speak euphemistically. They learn to create a pleasant impression and can be seductive in their presentation. These individuals have an intellectual aesthetic which strives to express ideas in an attractive way. They can be diplomatic but may withhold their real views in order to avoid the possibility of offending others.

This aspect indicates a tendency to suffer from a lack of intellectual self-esteem. Many natives attract people who either fail to appreciate their ideas or dislike their views. They run from those who might appreciate them. They cast their pearls before swine and feel stupid when others fail to appreciate them. These types tend to take criticism of their views personally and become defensive. This may be expressed in blunt speech or an arrogant stance. They may refuse to consider even minor alterations that might make their views more acceptable to others. This may make them appear smug or stubborn.

These natives enjoy intelligent, well-rounded conversation. They think wholistically, feel uncomfortable with incomplete thoughts, and like to tie things up. They either are attracted to platonic relationships or are non-communicative in their love. The former is more likely than the latter because these people are conditioned to believe that others like them more for their mind than for their body. Loving words, therefore, may replace physical love. These natives should be careful when they fall in love, because this aspect may induce them to think and perceive like the love object. These natives should also be aware of a tendency to see things the way one might like them to be rather than the way they really are.

This inconjunct might be good for writing, verbal communication or artistic pursuits. These natives have pleasant voices which might be suitable for phone communication or media work. The aspect also indicates an interest in music which, if reinforced elsewhere in the chart, might suggest talent. The ability to make a pleasant presentation might find success in sales or advertising. The ability to be tactful and put people at ease might be useful in public relations.

MERCURY INCONJUNCT MARS

The theme here is intellectual aggression. These natives are learning to think technically, speak directly and assert their views courageously. They are challenged to be less aggressive, more tactful and accept constructive criticism.

This aspect indicates a sharp, quick mind. These natives like to think for themselves and develop their own ideas. They have a knack for understanding the technical side of things, and seek crispness and clarity in thought and expression. Their perceptions are acute but they may not reveal what they see.

The Mercury-Mars inconjunct indicates difficulty in communication related to problems with aggression. These natives expect to be attacked for their views, which, in fact, often do create conflict. This leads to lying or dissembling in order to avoid unpleasantness. They may issue disclaimers in order to defuse the anticipated impact of their views. Some natives seem to attract verbal abuse, while others may feign ignorance for their own protection. Many of these people cannot stand to be contradicted. They tend to take criticism as a personal attack and react defensively with anger. A sharp and aggressive manner tends to preclude the exchange of ideas. Some natives cannot admit they are wrong and waste time and energy defending untenable positions. The inability to retreat forces them to respond to any challenge. A need to prove their daring leads to unwise actions.

There may be a tendency to substitute intellectual aggression for physical activity. Many natives substitute intellectual understanding for direct experience. They may fantasize about romance and heroism but find it hard to initiate activity. Many of these people have difficulty dealing with anger. The tendency is to express aggression indirectly, through wit or sarcasm. Some natives may kid or goad people sadistically, while others masochistically draw abuse to themselves through constant complaint. Some derive satisfaction by intentionally provoking others in order to get a rise out of them. This aspect might indicate a tendency to turn to physical activity in compensation for feelings of intellectual inferiority. The natives become the strong, silent types who let their actions speak for them. You may not know what they are thinking, but when they act they force others to reassess their attitudes.

This inconjunct permits these natives to develop the capacity for motivating people by challenging them to greater accomplishment. It might indicate supervisory talent. These same qualities also may be used in teaching or guidance counseling. The aspect indicates an ability to modify or re-evaluate work methods. This aspect also indicates potential talent for scientific or mathematical thought. The aggressive instinct expressed through intellectual channels suggests potential talent in law or debate. The aspect also indicates manual dexterity, and these natives may be able to find work as typists, court stenographers, word processors, machinists, mechanics or musicians.

MERCURY INCONJUNCT JUPITER

The theme here is knowledge v. wisdom. These natives are learning to communicate simply and assess new information accurately. They are challenged to listen to constructive criticism and to stop trying to impress others with their knowledge.

This aspect indicates an expansive and sociable nature. These natives want to be friendly, communicate and display their knowledge. Their friendships are based upon sharing of intellectual interests. They can be generous and encouraging. There is an ability to instill confidence in others, but because they are reluctant to speak frankly, they may create false optimism.

These natives have philosophical minds. They may be either liberal or orthodox and legalistic, but they have a strong drive for knowledge which seeks to comprehend the laws of life. They either are more interested in general principles than specific facts or may be walking encyclopedias with little perspective. Many natives lack faith in their own intellectual powers and, therefore, seek to cite authoritative sources. They really want to impress others and, therefore, may develop an extensive vocabulary and a wide scope of knowledge. This type may exaggerate, use large words or communicate in a pompous manner. There is a tendency to long-winded statements, which no one can follow. Once they start they don't know when to stop. This causes others to close off in boredom.

The Mercury-Jupiter inconjunct often indicates difficulties in communication due to distortion of perspective. Digressions and general discursiveness tend to create obstacles to understanding. The problem here is large concepts v. trivia, the forest v. the trees. These natives often express themselves in complex or involuted ways because they seek to avoid opposition. They tend to either exaggerate or minimize the importance of their ideas. They attract people who either overrate or belittle their intelligence. Some natives seek to maintain a standard of intellectual dignity and grandeur, but usually wind up being grandiose instead. They sometimes accomplish this at the expense of others because in the process of raising themselves up they put others down. Many natives remain silent in order to avoid revealing any lack of knowledge. Rather than ask questions, they may either try to fake it or avoid risking new projects. As a result, they can lose opportunities or find themselves in embarrassing situations.

This inconjunct is useful in all types of media work. Great satisfaction may be found in the field of education. These natives make good teachers because they can help others broaden their perspectives. An interest in knowledge and information might lead to library work. These people also might find success in law, where the concern for legalistic correctness can find its natural outlet. Other vocational possibilities might include the travel industry, clergy, fund raising or philanthropy.

MERCURY INCONJUNCT SATURN

The theme here is intellectual maturity. These natives are learning to think realistically and speak responsibly. They are challenged to stop discouraging others, accept constructive criticism and participate in the exploration of new ideas.

This aspect indicates a disciplined and scientific mind which strives to be rational, realistic and pragmatic. These natives learn to think before they speak and eventually develop the patience to take the time to think things through. They develop ideas by testing their validity and practicality. However, they may be so rigorous that they never have enough proof to satisfy their skepticism. They want to see things in concrete terms. Their thinking is traditional and conservative in at least some areas and they may be intellectually rigid and resistant to new ideas.

The Mercury-Saturn inconjunct indicates a tendency to measure oneself against impossibly high intellectual standards. This leads to fears of intellectual inferiority and incompetence, which causes these natives to become reserved. They start to think that they should speak only when they have something profound to say, usually pessimistic or discouraging. When they do have something important to say, they are forced by circumstances, and the need to be responsible, to wait interminably before they can express themselves. It is not unusual for these people to be faced with some form of censorship by unreasonable authorities. They learn that the practical result of speaking up is additional burdens or responsibilities, and this causes them to become even more circumspect in their speech.

Many natives tend to feel defensive over the quality and acceptability of their ideas. They unconsciously may fear ostracism for heretic views. They can be very sensitive to criticism, taking it as an attack upon their competence. Their predilection for slow, structured thought helps them to be thorough, but solitude is required for them to be at their best. This makes it difficult for them to respond to criticism extemporaneously. They develop an unapproachable manner which discourages challenge. One of their favorite tactics is to be both authoritative and impatient at the same time, which effectively denies others the time to speak or develop their thoughts. This may have the undesired effect of isolating these natives from any critical feedback.

This inconjunct can be appropriate for scientific or mathematical work. Natives with this aspect also make good teachers. In the literary field, the aspect can make for good editors or proofreaders. The Mercury-Saturn combination indicates a potential for discipline, which might help these people develop digital dexterity. Therefore, they may be good typists, court stenographers or musicians.

MERCURY INCONJUNCT URANUS

The theme here is intellectual independence. These natives are learning to challenge intellectual conformity, play the devil's advocate and rethink ideas on a basic level. They are challenged to accept constructive criticism, to be more tactful and less provocative.

These natives have inventive minds with a talent for solving puzzles. They tend to think abstractly and impersonally. They are intellectual nonconformists with a zany sense of humor. These natives seem to be on a different wavelength. They approach problems from a different perspective – sometimes brilliant, sometimes undisciplined.

The Mercury-Uranus inconjunct often indicates difficulties in communication due to rebelliousness. These natives are more interested in shocking people and overturning ideas than in communicating. They are attracted to unpopular, unusual, rebellious or radical ideas. There may be an attraction to rigid people who resist their ideas, and who misunderstand and dismiss their ideas as odd or eccentric. There is some validity in this, for their thinking is often perverse in at least some respects. These people love to upset others by playing the devil's advocate. They create shock and dismay every time they express their rebellious views. This reaction causes them to feel pressured to hide their true views, but they find it hard to hold their tongues. Many of them impulsively speak up regardless of the consequences. They seem to have a knack for voicing other people's private concerns. This makes them a prime target for gossip or slander.

This aspect indicates an ability to rethink things on a basic level. These natives attack issues at their roots. They shed light on old concepts and attempt to induce people to reconsider their views. They upset people by threatening their basic premises. There is the potential for helping others suspend their rational processes in order to receive new inspiration, but in order to do this, these natives must learn to communicate patiently in nonthreatening ways.

There may be intellectual competitiveness. A desire to be the best and most unique causes these natives to react to criticism with anxiety or rage. They may remain silent until they have something unusual or unique to contribute. They expect to be misunderstood or misrepresented. Their whole manner may be geared to putting others off. They may speak rapidly or with a disconnected cadence, or they cut others off before a thought is completed. These people speak before they think and later regret it. Some types may think so rapidly that they have too many thoughts to express clearly and as a result, may wind up being inexpressive or enigmatic.

This inconjunct lends itself to research. The desire to explore roots in order to reveal new facets of an issue might find an excellent outlet in psychology or in investigative reporting. An interest in the novel or innovative can be put to good use in proposal writing. The interest in solving problems might find its expression in computer programming. If they can develop the patience to attend to details. The urge for independence and nonconformity might find fruition in trade union work, where these people can challenge established concepts and conditions.

MERCURY INCONJUNCT NEPTUNE

The theme here is creative imagination. These natives are learning to trust intuition, use imagination and inspire others with their visions. They are challenged to think more realistically, communicate clearly and forego the temptation to escapism.

This aspect endows a good imagination and a talent for imagery and fantasy. These natives can develop the ability to move people through art, music, poetry or mystical vision. They can learn to use imagery to get their point across. These people can be highly receptive and impressionable, perhaps psychic. They also can be romantic and idealistic, qualities which may be so pronounced that they may cloud realistic perception or rational thought. These natives, therefore, are prone to fanciful or utopian ideals, which are bound to disappoint them.

The Mercury-Neptune inconjunct may indicate escapist tendencies. These people may be easily distracted, find concentration difficult, or just plain daydream. This makes them prone to mistakes for inattention tends to create misunderstandings. They must learn, therefore, to set fantasy aside in order to perceive more realistically. An eagerness to accept things on faith should be curtailed because of a vulnerability to deceit.

Many natives suffer from intellectual self-doubt and need reassurance of the validity of their views. Their intellectual uncertainty makes them vulnerable to counterclaims. They may react to criticism by vacillating in their beliefs. This makes it difficult for them to stick to decisions. Their undisciplined and unstructured thinking tends to foster confusion and unfounded fears. They may be forced, at times, to contend with other people's unfounded fears and beliefs. Their ambivalence causes them to send and receive double messages. Vague thinking leads to an ambiguous or confusing choice of words. It would be wise for these people to make clarity of expression a goal – otherwise they may be prone to being misunderstood or misrepresented by others.

This inconjunct lends itself to effective communication through suggestion, allusion or metaphor. These natives develop an ability to communicate indirectly, on subtle levels. The aspect may be fortunate for people in the entertainment industry: actors, musicians or creative writers especially. The image-making ability is excellent for poetry, advertising or other media work. These natives have mystical feelings that might be utilized in religious or spiritual pursuits. The ability to get people to accept obligations may be useful in charitable work.

MERCURY INCONJUNCT PLUTO

The theme here is obsessive thinking. These natives are learning to think analytically, share knowledge and let go of outmoded views. They are challenged to listen to others, be more flexible in their views and stop living by agendas.

This aspect indicates a good investigative and analytical mind. These natives possess a powerful sixth sense and a nose for the truth. Their senses are keen. They read others by picking up gut reactions. When they become interested in a project, they have the persistence to follow through. They are keenly perceptive but rarely reveal what they see. They are generally diplomatic and tactful, but can be devastatingly insightful when they want to be.

The Mercury-Pluto inconjunct indicates problems in communication related to intellectual insecurity. These natives may be intellectually rigid and find it difficult to accept criticism. They want to be sure of themselves and certain about their ideas before speaking. This may lead them to rehearse before doing so. They can be uncompromisingly dogmatic or attracted to doctrinaire people. Some natives have difficulty assimilating new ideas. An attachment to old ideas may create intellectual stagnation. Some types become so concerned about being misunderstood that they become reserved or uncommunicative. Others may be compulsive dissemblers who tell people what they want to hear in order to gain an advantage. Other types become so obsessed with being heard or under-stood that they become compulsive talkers. A curiosity and need to communicate may sometimes be a temptation to gossip.

There may be a problem in tolerating uncertainty or in adjusting to the unexpected. These natives want to be prepared in advance. Their need to live by agendas makes them unspontaneous. They want to control the flow of conversation or information in order to preclude any surprises. They try to understand others completely in order to be able to predict behavior or anticipate reactions. The need to know everything can make these natives oppressive in a close relationship. The challenge here is to let people be and accept them as they are.

This inconjunct usually indicates a potential for using words to great effect. These natives may develop an ability to use allusion or metaphor to good advantage. They also learn to use humor when presenting new information. These people have the potential to help others reassess their views and may make natural psychologists, actors, researchers or detectives. They also might become adept at propaganda, which can find successful application in advertising or literary fields. If these natives can let go of old ideas, they have the potential for self-renewal.

MERCURY INCONJUNCT ASC/DSC

The theme here is communication as the key to relationship. These natives are learning to share knowledge, listen to other people and communicate effectively. They are challenged to stop complaining, accept constructive criticism and resist the temptation to redundancy.

This aspect gives the potential for influencing others through the power of thought. These natives can develop a charismatic manner, and learn how to make effective presentations, which make unpalatable ideas acceptable. They learn that more flies are attracted with honey than with vinegar. They develop an ability to enlist support through tact, diplomacy and the proper choice of words. These natives usually have excellent perception and a good mind, but may doubt their intellectual capacity. This induces them to be cautious and thorough in approaching new ideas.

The Mercury-ASC/DSC inconjunct puts the emphasis upon obsessive thinking and communication. These natives want to be understood and heard by everyone, and need to have their intelligence acknowledged. They fear that people will misunderstand or misrepresent them. They want to express their views but also want to avoid criticism. This double bind may cause vacillation between verbosity and reticence.

There usually are strong ideas about money, sex or relationships. These natives may suffer economic repercussions when they reveal their views and may, therefore, learn to keep silent. They seem to attract people who are resistant to their ideas, and, consequently, remain silent in order to preclude jeopardizing their relationships. They have definite ideas about relationship, which keep them from seeing others clearly. They seek partners who conform to their notions and wind up deceiving themselves. They are attracted to those who fulfill their intellectual needs vicariously.

These natives may have difficulty dealing with criticism, or they may attract people who are intolerant of criticism. They use brusque speech in order to put others off. These natives can be resistant to the opinions of others. They may develop a fund of knowledge as a defense against other views. They can be so intellectually intimidating that they discourage frank and candid dialogue. This effectively isolates them and prevents them from learning from others.

This inconjunct, in its positive manifestations, can be useful for anyone who has to communicate with people. These natives might make effective speakers or writers. Their desire to communicate works to their advantage in sales, public relations, teaching and counseling. Their ability to make effective presentations might be useful in advertising professions.

MERCURY INCONJUNCT MC/IC

The theme here is resistance to intellectual authority. These natives are learning to rethink accepted beliefs, speak to authority figures and represent other people. They are challenged to overcome resentment, accept constructive criticism and avoid intellectual tyranny.

This aspect endows one with a good critical mind. These natives have a latent ability to understand both sides of an issue. There is a desire for knowledge and a need to challenge traditional beliefs. Their ability to speak both for the downtrodden and established authorities gives them the potential for developing much needed ideas of reform. These people seem to possess an uncanny talent for turning established ideas against each other and using other people's arguments to support their own causes. When presenting their case they sound authoritative and may, therefore, have a talent for legal matters.

The Mercury-MC/IC inconjunct tends to indicate rebellious thinking. These natives may be attracted to or foster unpopular ideas about life, society and the world. They are caught in the bind of rebellious opposition, and the need to seek permission to speak. There is a tendency to want the world to acknowledge the value of their views, but they are attracted to people who ignore or disrespect them, instead. They have difficulty in speaking to superiors, and present their ideas to authorities who refuse to listen. When these natives do get people to listen, they manage to sabotage their case, one way or another. These individuals may create problems for themselves whenever they speak up. Superiors seem to misrepresent their statements and use their words against them. Natives may, therefore, learn to withhold their true views from superiors, in order to protect themselves.

Career issues may be related to problems in communication. This means that, for these natives, worldly success is a function of their ability to communicate. The problem here is that these people tend to be very sensitive to criticism by family, authority, superiors and the community. They, therefore, feel pressured to present themselves diplomatically in order to avoid the severe reactions they fear. They feel pressured to maintain a reserved manner, but suffer the frustration of having to muzzle themselves. Some natives so resent having to be silent that they cannot restrain themselves. The desire to avoid criticism is doomed from the start by an outspoken manner. These people can be so brusquely outspoken that they alienate co-workers. An insensitivity to other's feelings often hinders their career advancement. If they attain a position of authority, they can become petty tyrants, if they aren't careful. They must develop tact and an ability to let things pass or rebellious discontent will occur.

These natives seem to have an unhealthy interest in other people's private affairs and tend to voyeuristic curiosity. They may pry into private lives, pass rumors or gossip about their neighbors. They need a taste of the same treatment before they learn the value of privacy. They, therefore, attract prying people who gossip about their private concerns. Gossip and slanderous rumor may sometimes create career or family problems for them. This eventually teaches them that minding one's own business is generally the wisest policy.

This inconjunct, at its best, helps these natives force society to reconsider its accustomed views. The aspect may make for a good researcher or reporter. Since these natives have a taste for communication and intellectual work, they might find success in writing or public relations. Empathy for the underdog helps these individuals give voice to social needs. This is useful for work in the social services. The ability to use established arguments (against each other) might indicate legal talent. They might make good counselors or lawyers. The desire for knowledge makes for interest in library science or history.

VENUS INCONJUNCT MARS

The theme here is the need to act v. the need to be liked. These natives are learning to act simply, assert their needs and put a realistic value on their services. They are challenged to forego the need to prove themselves and stop trying to win others over.

This aspect indicates a need to resolve the classic conflicts between the technical v. the aesthetic, perfection v. completion, form v. function, and specialization v. wholistic awareness. These natives feel a need to act simply and directly but also want to be creative and romantic. There is a struggle to improve themselves and perfect their skills, but much energy is wasted by trying to accomplish too much. They want to be activists but also want to be peacemakers. They may even wind up becoming fervent pacifists. There is often an excessive need to be liked. These natives tend to suffer from feelings of unworthiness, unlovability, and unattractiveness. They, therefore, become obsessed with winning others over. This may take the form of denial of aggressive needs, and may lead to difficulty in expressing anger, self-assertion, taking initiative or acting in one's own behalf. Some natives attempt to win love or appreciation through physical beauty, while others avoid the issue altogether. The former spend their energy on exercise, careful grooming and fashion, while the latter neglect their appearance and concern themselves with mental or spiritual pursuits. These people may attempt to win appreciation for their work but can't seem to accept it when it comes. Many of these natives cannot seem to relax or take a rest. They become workaholics because they would rather sublimate pleasure in work than stop and take satisfaction in their accomplishments. These natives may also find it difficult to barter or negotiate on their own behalf. They can't place a realistic value on their efforts, either finding it hard to ask for adequate renumeration or demanding excessive rewards.

The Venus-Mars inconjunct tends to indicate a distortion of material values relating to overindulgence or denial of physicality or pleasure. Many of these natives feel a strong need to develop their physical prowess, because they believe that strength and power will make them more attractive. They may become vain about their physical appearance or prowess. Romantic longings and a desire to demonstrate courage give these people strong powers of perseverance, especially in the face of pain. Some natives have insatiable sexual appetites which might lead to promiscuity, while other types may find release for their pent-up anger through sado-masochistic interests. Some types may batter love ones, while others may become victims of such treatment. The inability to express aggressive needs appropriately may inhibit the expression of love as well. Some natives might try to repress their physical needs. This often results in wide swings between indulgence and abstinence. The lack of moderation is the result of an inability to be comfortable with the physical satisfactions of life.

This inconjunct helps one find satisfaction in creative activity. These natives develop new creative methodologies and eventually perfect their aesthetic. They may become designers who find the right balance between technical, aesthetic and human considerations. The interest in sublimating aggression might lead to mediation or peace making careers. These natives will find daily exercise profitable. The interest in physical aesthetics might lead them to dance. They also might enjoy aesthetic/physical sports such as gymnastics or bodybuilding.

VENUS INCONJUNCT JUPITER

The theme here is development of social perspective. These natives are learning to accept love, assess value and understand the importance of appearance. They are challenged to develop intimate relationships and stop trying to impress others or buy them with generosity.

This aspect indicates a generous and expansive disposition. These natives can be gracious and charming as well as indulgent and wasteful. They encourage creative expression with their pocketbooks and especially favor large and expensive projects. They like to do favors and help others manage their affairs. Some natives, however, may become the recipients of others' generosity. These natives like to accumulate money and possessions, especially other people's. They seem to be able to demand favors. They have grandiose expectations, and do things in a big way. This aspect indicates a broad religious or philosophical spirit, so these natives also may enjoy metaphysical pursuits and entertainment with a spiritual theme.

This inconjunct can indicate a sense of failure related to a lack of self-esteem. These natives tend to lack faith in their own resources. They forego opportunities rather than risk failure. They tend to belittle themselves and expect others to undervalue them as well. They might abandon projects and fail in order to conform to others' expectations. This theme can sometimes take complex turns when other people don't undervalue them. These people may purposely fail rather than live up to the positive expectations of others. They also may have great difficulty in bartering or setting adequate fees for their services, either undervaluing themselves or overestimating other people's worth. The average types usually are undercompensated for their efforts. Some types, however, defensively overvalue themselves or belittle others, and tend to demand excessive rewards. The effect, in either case, is loss of opportunity because others react by questioning the natives' worth or rejecting their outrageous demands.

The Venus-Jupiter inconjunct often indicates problems in giving and accepting love due to feelings of unlovability or unattractiveness. These natives overestimate the importance of appearance and elevate it to the most important factor in social acceptance. Their belief that lovability depends upon attractiveness can make them vain. They may groom constantly in order to present themselves in the best light, while secretly belittling themselves. They may judge others by appearances as well, since these natives tend to judge the book by its cover and forget about the content. Some types feel so hopelessly unattractive that they give up and keep themselves plain.

Many of these natives feel a strong need to win others over, may try to buy love with generosity, and win appreciation by managing things or doing favors for people. Other natives suffer from fears of abandonment, which makes it difficult for them to trust and make emotional commitments. They find it so hard to accept intimate love that they may reject it when it is offered. These people are attracted, instead, to those who withhold love or offer it conditionally. They may pursue people who will abandon them. Some types deceive themselves by forming relationships with people in other cities. This long-distance love has two striking features: it guarantees lack of intimate closeness and also serves as an excuse against forming close relationships with others who are nearby.

Lack of perspective may make these natives complacent, self-righteous or smug. They can be legalistic and orthodox, and may refuse to attempt anything which might compromise their dignity. Stuffiness, therefore, prevents them from enjoying themselves because they dare not be lighthearted or playful.

This inconjunct indicates an ability to manage and administrate. It forces the development of a perspective which permits the accurate appraisal of others. It indicates a coming to terms with the material side of life, and, therefore, can be a good aspect for a stockbroker or business manager. It also is a good aspect for a producer of artistic projects. An interest in attractive appearance might permit these natives to excel in advertising or in packaging.

VENUS INCONJUNCT SATURN

The theme here is maturity in social intercourse. These natives are learning to be realistic in their affections, responsible in love and set a realistic value on their efforts. They are challenged to avoid the impulse to win others over by taking on unnecessary burdens and stop accepting appreciation in lieu of money.

This aspect indicates conservative tastes, a discriminating manner and a finely attuned aesthetic eye. These natives love quality and despise mediocrity. They have serious tastes and severe standards which value the mature and restrained. Moderation is their ideal, and it is pursued in both private and public relationships. This sometimes may be the result of inhibition rather than restraint. These natives can be very tactile and skin sensitive, and also may find it difficult to tolerate high levels of pleasure. They may justify the avoidance of personal pleasure by engaging in spiritual disciplines which demand the denial of material satisfactions.

There can be difficulty in relationship due to a sense of unworthiness. Many of these natives have a Cinderella complex, which makes them feel unlovable and unattractive. They may put the material needs of others ahead of their own, and accept burdens and hardships, only to find that others are unappreciative. This leaves them feeling used and taken advantage of, but they don't know how to reach out for love. If love should be offered, responsibility is used as an excuse for avoiding involvement. Perhaps they really are avoiding the responsibility of love. Many of these natives feel unattractive and worry about the impression they make. They groom themselves carefully to forestall the aging process, but may not age gracefully. Other types give up and look prematurely old. Many of these natives try to win others over by accepting responsibilities. They especially try to please sceptical authority figures who, naturally, withhold the respect they seek. These natives tend to be caught between the desire to be liked and the need to be respected. As a consequence, they may have difficulty in setting limits or asserting authority. They begin to change once they discover that this behavior gets them neither love nor respect.

Many of these people suffer from low self-esteem. They feel a strong need to prove their maturity and responsibility. They measure themselves against high standards and then worry about their competence. The sense of inferiority attracts them to people who disrespect them. They then get caught up in trying to win respect from people who withhold it. Getting caught up in a work ethic allows them to bypass the anxiety associated with pleasure. Pleasurable activities may not be pursued because time or money might be wasted. These people may become so perfectionistic that they cannot be satisfied with mere excellence. They tend to be penny-wise and pound-foolish, frugal to the point of miserliness, but will pay excessive prices in pursuit of perfection. These natives also have difficulty bartering their services realistically, either overcharging or accepting minimal fees. They may be forced to wait a long time before they are finally compensated.

The Venus-Saturn inconjunct indicates difficulty in participating in the mainstream of social life. Many of these natives feel lonely and isolated. A pessimistic and discouraging attitude makes it difficult for them to enjoy themselves. They can be socially passive and awkward in groups, and need time to unwind and feel comfortable with others. Some of these types have barriers between themselves and others. Excuses for the barriers may be age, social inexperience or pressure of tradition, but the problem is usually related to fear. The key to breaking this estrangement is in the development of the ability to comfort others and receive comforting in return.

This inconjunct helps to develop the ability to see the world realistically. These natives ultimately learn when to be defensive and when to relax and enjoy life. The need for economy teaches them how to make trade-offs between cost and quality. This may lead to success in administration or management. These natives might make good accountants, budgeters or financial analysts. Their discipline applied to art might lead to success in mastering a musical instrument. Their tactility can find useful application in manual work, sculpture or massage. These natives also may consider careers in the health field.

VENUS INCONJUNCT URANUS

The theme here is appreciation of originality. These natives are learning to value independence, appreciate individuality and set a realistic price on their services. They are challenged to resist the pressure to conform, to be more considerate and stop provoking others.

This aspect indicates unusual tastes and different values. These natives have their own aesthetic, which leans toward the abstract and impersonal. They want to be different. They weary of the usual and enjoy the excitement of the novel or unexpected. They can be extraordinarily creative, especially in the solution of artistic problems. They have an ability to go to the basics of a situation and come up with new alternatives. This may, however, make others feel insecure.

There is a tendency toward indirect aggression. These natives can be rebellious in passive aggressive ways. Tension and anxiety seem to be their constant companions. They create instability and then feel uncomfortable. They upset people by shaking them out of their indolence and complacency. The desire to enlighten others through shock creates problems in relationships. As a result, these natives may have difficulty getting close to others. Anxiety and an inability to relax may create intimacy problems. Difficulty with pleasure anxiety may lead to sexual problems. Some types may prefer platonic to romantic love, while other types may develop bizarre or perverse sexual tastes, which are essentially forms of autoeroticism.

The Venus–Uranus inconjunct indicates a concern with personal appearance and social acceptance. These natives tend to feel pressured to conform in order to be liked. They may, therefore, hide their differences in order to avoid attracting attention. Some may be extraordinarily beautiful and charming, but most feel unattractive. Some natives go to great lengths to conform to current images of beauty, while other natives accentuate their differences through style or cosmetics. A good number of these people may be unreliable or inconsistent in love, may have difficulty in accepting love when it is offered. They have to forego dwelling upon their ugly duckling past if they are to find fulfillment in the present.

This aspect indicates problems with self-esteem. These natives worry about unfavorable comparisons with others. They want to excel but may fear standing out from the norm. They want to avoid being dismissed as eccentric. Since it is difficult for them to prove their worth, they find it hard to barter their services, either accepting minimal compensation or overcharging. These natives want to engage in unusual activities, but financial pressures force them to conform. They may eventually learn to conform outwardly while still maintaining individuality in their private affairs.

This inconjunct ultimately forces these natives to apply their creative talents within the bounds of social acceptance. They learn how to create interest and excitement without upsetting or offending people. This aspect, therefore, can be useful for someone in advertising, sales or promotion. These natives also may have a great deal of artistic talent, especially for abstract or one-of-a-kind projects. They may have a knack for creating new styles and encouraging new aesthetic trends, and may find design to be a fulfilling outlet for their talents.

VENUS INCONJUNCT NEPTUNE

The theme here is love v. obligation. These natives are learning to accept relationship commitments, make their desires clearer and express their inspirations creatively. They are challenged to overcome self-doubt, resist escapist tendencies and avoid ambivalence in their affections.

This aspect indicates a kind and sympathetic nature. These natives can be quite empathetic. Their charismatic natures permit them to soothe and comfort others with their presence. They tend to have strong mystical leanings and are attracted to the spiritual and intangible. The idealistic nature expresses itself in romantic longings. A talent for creative imagination allows them to inspire others with new images.

There is a tendency toward a great deal of confusion and delusion in relationship. These people feel unlovable and unattractive. Some natives take great pains to improve their looks with an overdose of cosmetics, while other natives do nothing to enhance their appearance. Most of these people have problems with self-doubt and need constant reassurance from others. A need to be liked by everyone causes them to react to any nuance of displeasure with despair. This makes them vulnerable to the vicissitudes of others' feelings. They may, therefore, attract people who prey upon this vulnerability by withholding love or appreciation, or by granting it conditionally. These natives may go to great lengths to win others over, including acceptance of obligation or self-sacrifice. Self-doubt is reflected in their ambivalent attitude toward others. Uncertainty and indecision cause problems in communication related to the giving and receiving of double messages. These natives can be fickle in their affections. Unrealistic desire induces them to pursue those who would deny them love and avoid those who would love them. They must be careful to avoid attracting people who might love them for ulterior purposes.

The Venus–Neptune inconjunct indicates problems in self-worth related to confusion and illusion. These natives find it hard to assess their own value. They attract people who confuse them with ambivalent messages. Self-doubt causes their shaky self-esteem to vacillate according to other people's feelings. Their tentative and uncertain nature seeks reassurance from others. They may seek to win sympathy rather than make straightforward demands. This creates problems when it comes time for them to bargain or barter their services. They don't seem to value money or be able to utilize it wisely and, therefore, find it difficult to set an appropriate fee for their efforts. They may settle for IOU's instead. This may lead others to resent them, because no one likes to feel obligated.

A strong escapist nature gives these natives a rich fantasy life, which can impede real fulfillment. Their daydreams about love cause them to harbor unrealistic expectations about others. An absentminded nature may subvert productive effort. Some types may turn to drugs or alcohol for release from the pressures of daily life. They are better advised to use music or meditation for the same purpose.

This inconjunct indicates an ability to enjoy art, music, photography, dance or poetry. These natives may have a talent for writing or for the theater. They might find satisfaction in the cosmetic industry. Their image-making ability can find expression in advertising. The interest and sympathy in others might indicate potential for fulfillment in the healing professions. These natives also might have a talent for fund raising or find satisfaction in spiritual pursuits. A more mundane use for escapist tendencies can lead them to work as bartenders or travel agents.

VENUS INCONJUNCT PLUTO

The theme here is love v. control. These people are learning to let go of old satisfactions, live in the present and accept the uncertainty of love. They are challenged to overcome obsessiveness, be more flexible in their affections and forego the need to win others over.

This aspect indicates a potential talent for husbanding resources and making use of the past. These natives have a latent ability to utilize discarded assets for new creative projects. A conservative nature urges them to recycle rather than discard. Their talent for aesthetic analysis permits them to appreciate the potential for transforming old material into pleasing new forms. The need is to fulfill and their aesthetic tends toward wholeness and balance.

This aspect indicates relationship difficulties related to feelings of unlovability and unattractiveness. Some of these natives can be obsessive about their appearance. A belief that beauty begets loves makes them work hard to perfect their appearance. These people often have difficulty tolerating minor flaws. They can be compulsively neat and find it hard to tolerate any type of disorder. They can be superficially attracted to and judge others on the basis of mere appearance. Other natives can be completely neglectful of their appearance, untidy and find it difficult to maintain order for any length of time. Most of these natives obsess about their relationships. Their feelings of unlovability often create dependency problems. The need for security causes them to obsess about every aspect of the relationship, until it is destroyed. They seem to dwell constantly upon "what if" thoughts. Their fear of change makes them want to understand every nuance so that they can be prepared for any eventuality. They want to know what to expect and how to act, but events rarely work out that way. They wind up badgering loved ones with questions and prying into their motivations with an intensity that borders on oppressiveness.

An obsessive need to be liked by everyone can impel these natives to do everything in their power to win others over. This may take the form of passivity, charm or catering to others. This permits people to take advantage of them by withholding love or granting it conditionally. Some natives, however, learn to use this aspect to manipulate others through appearance, charm or the conditional granting of love or affection.

The Venus-Pluto inconjunct indicates problems related to lack of self-esteem. These natives have difficulty acting or taking initiative because they can't seem to make demands. They feel that they have to earn the right to relax or be happy. An inability to assert themselves or make monetary demands makes it difficult for them to bargain. This means that they often overpay as well as fail to get their money's worth. Some natives, however, are driven to bargain by an obsessive need to get as much as they can for as little as possible. This aspect also indicates difficulty in bartering services for appropriate fees. The average native often undercharges and works for appreciation, which is rarely forthcoming. Some natives, however, set outrageous fees for their services and wind up driving people away.

A strong need to control people, circumstances and events causes many of these natives to be stilted and inflexible. A difficulty in adjusting to change can make them stubborn. The tendency to live by agendas takes the spontaneity and fun out of life. They may spoil things by forcing them to fit preinclinations. These natives can be uncomfortable with imperfection and can't seem to leave things pending. The need for completeness demands closure. Some natives demand the gratification of ending. In athletics or politics, this may manifest as a killer instinct. In daily life, it usually means that these people persevere until they finish the job.

This inconjunct forces a coming to terms with the importance and unimportance of appearance. A kind heart may be more important than superficial attractiveness, but beauty does enhance the quality of life. These natives have the potential for finding fulfillment in theater, writing, music or art. The ability to create a pleasant or seductive presentation may make them good in sales or advertising. Some natives develop an ability to barter or negotiate on behalf of others and become good agents. Other natives may become good at money management and find opportunities in banking or the stock market.

VENUS INCONJUNCT ASC/DSC

The theme here is satisfaction in daily life. These natives are learning to be more loving, show appreciation and value attractive appearance. They are challenged to assert their needs, stop living vicariously and resist the desire to win others over.

This aspect indicates difficulty in self-assertion due to an overwhelming need to feel liked by everyone. Feelings of unlovability seem to be the major psychological force which motivates these natives to try to win others over. This allows people to take advantage of them by giving love or appreciation conditionally. Many of these natives try very hard to please people but find, instead, that they are taken for granted. They pursue people who withhold love, and avoid those who would love them. They seek appreciation but can't accept praise when it is given. Feelings of unlovability may sometimes take the form of acceptance of unhappiness and pleasure denial. Some natives have difficulty tolerating pleasure and subvert their happiness by turning away from basic satisfactions. Other natives accept a pleasure-denying life style as a form of religious or philosophical discipline.

The Venus-ASC/DSC inconjunct puts the emphasis upon appearances. Fears or feelings of unattractiveness cause these natives to be concerned with making a good impression. They tend to develop a charming facade and attractive manner, learn how to give people pleasure, and put them at ease. They may take great pains in grooming themselves because they believe that popularity depends upon beauty. They put the emphasis on packaging, and tend to judge others on the basis of surface appearance. Some natives, however, may express this aspect in a very different manner: a feeling of unattractiveness may be so strong that they give up and refuse to take even minor steps to enhance their appearance. These natives can be physically plain and socially awkward.

This aspect indicates problems in relationship due to difficulty in giving and accepting love. Feelings of unlovability in this case translate into unlovingness. These natives tend to pick partners who cannot or will not love them. Aberrations of the pleasure principle lead to either an inability to tolerate pleasure or an insatiable appetite for it. Problems related to mutuality of fulfillment lead to schisms in relationship. Lack of love sometimes leads to addiction to sweets, and orality replaces genitality. Feelings of unlovability leads to possessiveness and dependency. Attachment to money and possessions creates marital problems.

There may be difficulties in business and social life due to a lack of self-esteem. These natives have difficulty making demands and setting an appropriate value on their efforts. Some types compensate for feelings of unworthiness by becoming obsessed with financial worth. They worry about inconsequentials and become penny-wise and pound-foolish. Avarice becomes all important, and money becomes the major stumbling block in their relationships. They may marry for money or attract partners who seek them out for financial security. Frugality or wastefulness becomes the issue that creates disharmony and division. Separation reinforces feelings of unworthiness and makes them even more materialistic.

This inconjunct ultimately forces these natives to learn how to create an attractive presentation. They may excel in sales or packaging. Their aesthetic sense can be an asset in the arts, and their ability to make a favorable impression can be useful in public relations. The concern for value and worth ultimately teaches them how to handle money and they might gravitate toward careers in investment or finance. Their ability to put people at ease can find application in counseling, especially marital counseling.

VENUS INCONJUNCT MC/IC

The theme here is acceptance of social rewards. These natives are learning to make social demands, barter their services and use pleasant appearance as an asset. They are challenged to overcome resentment, avoid spite and stop trying to appease authority figures.

This aspect indicates career and social problems related to feelings of unlovability. These natives want to be liked by everyone, but especially need the acknowledgment of authority figures. They may, therefore, attempt to ingratiate themselves with superiors through flattery or appeasement. Although they work hard to win others over, it is hard for these natives to accept appreciation. They seek favors and praise from superiors, but these people wind up being taken for granted, and tend to be unappreciated at work.

There can be concern about being unattractive. While some natives may groom themselves carefully and use appearance as a career asset, other types can lose career opportunities because of their plain appearance. The former may become very vain while the latter accept their plainness with resignation. The former types may pursue pleasure while the latter seem to be asking for permission to have fun while resenting those who would grant it. Both types seem to have difficulty expressing love to parents and family. They keep their love so private that no one knows it exists. They may, thus, appear more platonic than passionate.

This inconjunct indicates career problems stemming from a lack of self-esteem. Self-worth is directly linked to work and career. They want to be suc cessful but also want to be liked by both inferiors and superiors. As a consequence, they may lack the aggressiveness to get to the top. This behavior may sometimes be misinterpreted by superiors as disinterest or lack of drive. Most of these natives have difficulty bartering their services for an appropriate price and consequently are underpaid. Some natives, however, compensate for feelings of low self-esteem by demanding excessive rewards. Many feel uncomfortable with authority. They either undermine it, or enjoy the exercise of power at other people's expense.

The Venus-MC/IC inconjunct sometimes indicates problems related to repression of pleasure. These natives may resent having to restrain playful impulses in deference to family or authority. They defer their own happiness and become jealous of other people's fun. As a consequence, they may learn to take satisfaction in spitefulness. Some natives develop a taste for revenge, while other types use voyeuristic curiosity as a means of vicarious satisfaction.

This inconjunct ultimately forces these natives to develop a concern for other people's happiness. It helps them develop a balanced approach to the problems of aesthetics, value and authority. This aspect, therefore, suggests possible vocational talent in the arts as well as in finance. These people eventually might develop an interest in handling money, which might find useful application in accounting, budgeting, economics or investment counseling. Their essentially peaceful nature may find satisfaction in mediation.

MARS INCONJUNCT JUPITER

The theme here is risk-taking. These natives are learning to organize activity, assess new procedures and motivate others. They are challenged to stop trying to prove their courage or intimidate others.

This aspect indicates a powerful need to prove oneself. These natives have a gambling instinct and a need for adventure. They want to be strong and seek to demonstrate their courage. Some might become explorers or daredevils, while other types may indulge in promiscuous adventures. Those who actualize these needs develop an ability to stand up for their beliefs and fight for their rights, which makes them natural leaders. The combination of initiative, courage and hard work enables them to take the huge risks which lead to great opportunities. The average types, however, find it difficult to fulfill these yearnings. A lack of confidence in their powers causes them to avoid the challenges which would develop their abilities. They tend to lack the initiative to take advantage of opportunities and abandon projects which entail risk. Success eventually comes when they learn to focus upon fulfillment of their own needs instead of resisting other people's expectations.

There often are difficulties with aggression. Some natives are over-aggressive, while others can't seem to assert themselves. The overaggressive types have very little patience and can't seem to tolerate frustration. They need to act, even if the action is premature or rash. Their forcefulness may turn to abusiveness, if they aren't careful. These people can be prone to violence when thwarted. The passive types tend to internalize their aggressive instincts and suffer from fatigue low energy or depression. They may be attracted to strong, impatient people who eventually abuse them. Both types have difficulty achieving intimacy in close relationships. They either run from people, use abuse as a barrier to closeness, or get involved with people in another town.

The Mars-Jupiter inconjunct indicates a strong need to impress people through some action or activity. This adds impetus to the need to develop strength or demonstrate physical prowess. These natives may, therefore, work very hard and set an example for others. They can be very generous in helping others with their tasks by pitching in, lending a hand and helping others organize their efforts. These natives act with dignity and stand by others in a crisis, but tend to attract fair-weather friends who abandon them in times of need.

This aspect indicates obstacles to success due to lack of perspective. These natives tend to misjudge their own and other people's prowess. They either badly overrate or underrate people, and belittle those they should respect. A tendency to misjudge tasks is another problem. They must learn to be more realistic in the assessment of their projects because this is a major obstacle to success. Sometimes, they underestimate the required effort and then give up when things become difficult. At other times, they overestimate the task and give up before even starting. A tendency to abandon projects in midstream is another obstacle to achievement. These natives must learn to slow down and attain a broader perspective before they jump into things. However, once they begin, they must persist because their lack of perseverance is a major problem. Some types have another impediment to achievement: rigid rule following and legalistic thinking which enmeshes them in red tape. They eventually learn that some informality or rule bending is necessary in order to overcome bureaucratic paralysis.

This inconjunct endows one with high energy. These natives have a great need for activity. One way of fulfilling this need is through physical activities such as sports, heavy exercise or dancing. Vocational outlets may include law, physical therapy or police work. Additional outlets might include gambling, auto racing or skydiving. These people make good leaders if they can cope with frustration.

MARS INCONJUNCT SATURN

The theme here is responsible action. These natives are learning to be patient, realistic and thorough in their activities. They are challenged to overcome inhibition, take more risks and avoid pessimism.

This aspect is an indicator of activity influenced by a burdensome sense of responsibility. These natives want acknowledgment for their efforts, especially from authority figures. The need to be taken seriously causes them to act with discipline and restraint. They approach their tasks pragmatically and prefer conservative solutions to problems. Hard work and acceptance of responsibility becomes the means for proving their maturity. Unfortunately, this attracts immature and irresponsible people, some of whom are authority figures, who create hardships by shirking their responsibilities. These natives may become so bogged down by other people's burdens that they have no time or energy to attend to their own projects. Responsibility, thus, either straitjackets them or forces them to act against their desires. These natives may sometimes be thrown into challenging situations without warning or preparation because of other people's shortcomings. They learn on the job and develop practical, economical methods. If they aren't careful, they may wind up instructing superiors, who then claim the credit for themselves.

The Mars–Saturn inconjunct indicates a tendency toward restrained aggression. These natives have good control of their passions. They can be determined, persistent and very set in their ways. There is a tendency to simmer and stew rather than to show anger openly. They are hard to provoke but can explode when frustration becomes too much for them. A weakness for jealousy and vengefulness can lead them to violence. They set limits, draw the line and issue ultimatums. Many natives, however, do not even have this explosive outlet for their passions. Not only do they avoid expressing anger, but they also fear competition and retreat from challenge. They either become chronic complainers or develop serious illnesses.

There may be a hindrance of activity due to obstruction and delay. These natives seem to be plagued by bad timing. They either jump into things prematurely or are slow to take initiatives. Some types act first and repent later, while other types rue their lack of action. Most natives worry too much and lose options because they hesitate too long. Many of these people feel hampered by tradition and discouraged by high standards. They often have to endure interminable delays before they can act, and are forced by circumstances to develop patience and plan their actions carefully.

This inconjunct may be useful in highly disciplined pursuits such as dancing or in mastering a musical instrument. These natives' ability to apply themselves physically may find application in manual labor, carpentry, gardening, auto mechanics, etc. Those with white-collar jobs might pursue such activity at home by attending to home repair. Their ability to attend to detail can find useful application in graphic design. This aspect also may be used in work planning and development of efficient economical procedures.

MARS INCONJUNCT URANUS

The theme here is independent action. These natives are learning to act quickly, assert their independence and develop original methodology. They are challenged to avoid impulsiveness, be less rebellious and stop provoking others.

This aspect indicates a misuse of physical powers related to feelings of anxiety. These natives have very strong feelings about being special in a physical way. They have high levels of energy which demand practical channels of expression. Many types have difficulty finding suitable outlets for their energies. They come to fear their aggressive urges, project a docile facade, and can be reluctant to take initiatives or assert themselves. They may fear violence and have difficulty expressing anger. Sexual inhibition may be present. These people can be perversely rebellious or passively aggressive. They also can be intellectually aggressive. They try to prove themselves exceptional through hard work and diligence, but may have to live with anxiety. Other natives use their energy quite differently, acting quickly and spontaneously. Rashness, impatience and lack of forethought tends to make them accident-prone. They accept challenges and try to prove their strength and courage. Promiscuity may be a way for them to prove their sexual prowess. They may have difficulty in tolerating frustration, and may resort to force to accomplish their ends. These people can be abusive in relationships if they aren't careful.

The Mars-Uranus inconjunct indicates a compulsion to act in unconventional ways. These natives take original or unique approaches to their tasks, do things their own way and experiment with new methods. They have trouble with conservative people who treat new procedures with suspicion. These natives often are forced to defend themselves against accusations of eccentricity. They feel pressured to conform to traditional methods and must be prepared to accept derisive criticism if they resist. They have little choice, however, for submission stifles their individuality. These people approach problems differently: they seek root causes instead of merely attending to symptoms. This upsets people because it challenges their basic ways. These natives are, therefore, compelled to act independently without support or understanding from others. They are often the only ones with the courage to act. Those natives who conform and act conventionally attract unconventional or rebellious types. They are, thus, forced to stabilize the turmoil created by their opposites.

There may be an irrepressible rebellious streak which often manifests as erratic or unreliable behavior. Many of these people secretly wish to shock or upset others with their actions or initiatives. They distrust authorities and assert themselves by rebelling at every opportunity. Erratic behavior becomes a way of rebellion, but the price of this is loss of effectiveness due to inconsistency and short-lived impulses. These natives resist discipline because they see it as oppressive. This puts them in a double bind because they need discipline to excel.

This inconjunct indicates a need for aggressive outlets such as competitive sports. These natives might excel in creative arenas, or find satisfaction in redesigning out-moded procedures. Their aggressive urges may find outlets in police work, the military, firefighting, etc. Their rebellious streak can be well used in trade-union work. The planetary symbolism suggests that this energy, tempered with patience, can find expression in psychic work, healing, acupuncture, dentistry or surgery.

MARS INCONJUNCT NEPTUNE

The theme here is imaginative action. These natives are learning to define tasks, fulfill commitments and develop motivating ideals. They are challenged to be more direct, overcome self-doubt and avoid escapist tendencies.

This aspect indicates a tendency to inaction due to indecisiveness and uncertainty. These natives want to act in creative, imaginative ways but don't know how to take practical measures. Their openness to new possibilities permits them to experiment with new procedures but lack of consistency undermines their effectiveness. Many of these people have difficulty making decisions. Ambivalence and self-doubt preclude initiative and inhibit action. Vacillation misdirects or scatters their energies and causes confusion. Self-doubt leads them to question their own powers and to seek reassurance from others. This induces people to lose confidence in them as well. Some types confuse instructions and misunderstand procedures. Other types make false starts and have difficulty sticking to a method. Vacillation and inattentiveness cause unnecessary complexity. Most natives are too easily distracted from their efforts and seem weak or irresolute. These people swing from assertion to passivity and self-reliance to passive dependency. They must learn to focus their energies and persevere in order to act effectively or accomplish anything.

The Mars-Neptune inconjunct indicates a tendency to act in accordance with romantic or fanciful ideas. These natives tend to indulge in heroic or romantic fantasies which have no realistic basis. An attraction to

Utopian ideals spurs them to act, but they are ultimately defeated and disillusioned. Many natives have a tendency to initiate activities on the basis of unfounded beliefs. Projects begun this way usually turn out to be impractical. These people, therefore, must learn to analyze the practicality of projects before beginning an effort. Some types act or refrain from action on the basis of imagined threats or deluded ideas. Irrational fears may cause them to strike out against others. Other types attract deluded or irrational people who may strike out against them. The unrealistic activities of some natives border on self-destructiveness. They think they are being martyrs but are more likely to be masochists.

There may be a major concern with avoidance of escapism and fulfillment of commitment. These natives must be careful, for daydream and fantasy replace action and inattention causes accidents. Some natives can be absentminded and forgetful of methods and procedures, while others dissipate their energies through drugs, alcohol or escapist pursuits. The more mature types come to take commitments seriously and act accordingly. The problem is that they may take it too seriously. These natives tend to get tied up in obligations which hamper their freedom of action. Some are forced to act against their desires, while others are required to avoid action. The net effect, however, is the same for either: loss of personal freedom through involuntary acceptance of burdensome responsibility. These people must learn to say NO or they will be easy prey for others who take advantage of their sympathies.

This inconjunct endows one with creative inspiration and an ability to act imaginatively. These natives possess a natural sense of the rhythms of activity and a latent talent for visualizing movement. This gives them a potential for excellence in dance, choreography or sports. The average native might find satisfaction in the release of energies through jogging, swimming, folk dancing, etc. The ability to anticipate action makes them good tacticians or strategists. Coaching might be one outlet for this aspect, scheduling of events might be another. Some natives may make good use of this aspect through volunteer work, counseling or fund raising.

MARS INCONJUNCT PLUTO

The theme here is transformative activity. These natives are learning to analyze activity, revise procedures and use diplomacy. They are challenged to avoid obsessive activity, overcome the temptation to prove themselves and be less set in their ways.

This aspect indicates a hard-working and persistent nature. These natives can be persevering but sometimes are merely stubborn and rigid. Compulsiveness keeps them constantly busy but they can be very set in their ways. They are attracted to agendas and like to follow well-defined procedures. Inflexibility makes it difficult to adapt to new situations. They rigidly apply preprogrammed methods even though those methods may be inappropriate. An obsession with work makes it difficult for them to take a rest. The desire to prove themselves through hard work permits others to manipulate them into accepting difficult or unpleasant tasks. Many of these types have difficulty initiating new projects because they dwell upon past activities. Other types find it difficult to work cooperatively and get into power struggles with colleagues or superiors. The key to effectiveness is flexibility and adaptability, and it is important to learn openness to new methods and procedures.

The Mars-Pluto inconjunct indicates a powerful need to prove oneself physically. These natives are attracted to or fascinated by strength and power. Some become obsessed with developing physical prowess and demonstrating courage. They are people of action who make assertion and initiative a way of life. They become diehard competitors who cannot accept defeat. Their obsession with winning makes it difficult for them to back down or retreat, even when wrong. A need to prove their daring makes them easy prey for people who manipulate them through challenge. These natives can't stand to be thwarted and can become violent when frustrated. Anger and intimidation become manipulative tools for maintaining their dominance. Promiscuity may be a way for them to prove their sexual prowess, and violent abuse a way for them to maintain dominance in relationships. Other natives repress and come to fear their aggressive urges. These types can't seem to act, take initiative or compete. They repress their sexuality and fear violence, and may attract aggression, violence or abuse if they aren't careful. They must learn to express anger appropriately, for inhibition may cause health problems such as depression, headaches, backaches, hemorrhoids or colitis.

There may be a resistance to change due to a fear of uncertainty. These natives seem to be motivated by a powerful fear of the unknown. They like the status quo and go out of their way to frustrate change. They can be unyielding and doctrinaire about procedures. They plan their activities carefully and attempt to anticipate all eventualities. These people want to know what to expect so that they can be forearmed. They want to know how others will act so that they can preprogram their reactions accordingly. This dogmatic behavior spills over into relationships. They try to control and dominate people in order to preclude unexpected attack. The need to be absolutely certain of people makes these individuals want to know everything about others' activities. This has the effect of oppressing people and driving them away.

This inconjunct develops a great deal of energy that demands a suitable outlet. Possible avenues of expression are physical labor such as carpentry, gardening, athletics, mountain climbing, etc. The law or the military might be one way of utilizing this energy vocationally. Healing, medicine and X-ray analysis may be other ways. This aspect also can find application in motivational research, work planning, methods analysis or psychology.

MARS INCONJUNCT ASC/DSC

The focus here is daily activity. These natives are learning to work hard, act simply and assert themselves. They are challenged to stop trying to prove themselves, avoid abusiveness and forego redundant activity.

This aspect indicates an overconcern with proving oneself through physical means. Some natives want to develop their physical abilities and demonstrate courage. Their romantic nature admires heroism and invites risk. Fear of being perceived as cowardly makes them prove themselves by accepting dares and leaves them open to manipulation by people who challenge them to act. They can be physically active and very hard working, their efforts often are taken for granted. The need to prove themselves sexually may lead to promiscuity. The tendency to overdo things makes their actions redundant. They must learn not to waste their energies on unnecessary tasks. Some natives internalize their needs for physicality and substitute a rich fantasy life for activity. These types can be passive, ineffectual or fearful. Repressed energy leads to depression and fatigue. Lack of energy leads to lack of effort and feelings of unaccomplishment. Physical activity in the form of sports can be the means for these people to get out of the doldrums.

The Mars-ASC/DSC inconjunct indicates relationship difficulties related to problems in expressing aggressive instincts. These natives either are very aggressive and abusive in relationship, or passive and inhibited. The former have difficulty handling frustration and may become quarrelsome or violent. The latter have difficulty expressing anger directly and resort to constant complaint. These types inhibit their anger to preserve relationships, but can be cranky and discontented. Their whining and complaining borders on abuse and may provoke others to retaliate angrily. They often are attracted to angry or aggressive people who offer them vicarious release for their aggressive instincts. These natives fear violence but provoke quarrels with partners anyway, especially over money matters. Sexual incompatibility and lack of initiative are additional pitfalls in relationship. If these natives are lucky, they will attract partners who light a fire under them and force them out of their passivity.

This tendency to react either too passively or too aggressively creates difficulties due to inappropriate action. The passive types are easily intimidated, and back away from action while allowing others to have free reign. These natives lose out in life through default, and may pay a physical penalty in the form of ailments of one sort or another. The active types tend to be impatient, overeager, impulsive, competitive or challenging. They are action oriented, and desirous of accomplishment. These natives assert themselves with a heavy hand, or overreact in general. Some can become obsessed with winning, or find it difficult to tolerate defeat. They can't handle frustration well and may resort to force to accomplish their goals.

This inconjunct eventually leads to the development of leadership ability. These natives acquire a sense of self-reliance which makes others look to them for direction. Their physical needs can be served by active exercise or sports. Vocational indications include manual activities such as plumbing or carpentry. These people also might work in the health services area as doctors, chiropractors, acupuncturists, surgeons or dentists. Combative needs might be served in work areas which involve conflict or negotiation.

MARS INCONJUNCT MC/IC

The theme here is assertion of authority. These natives are learning to act simply, assert leadership and motivate others. They are challenged to forego resentment, be more flexible and overcome the temptation to use force.

This aspect indicates a need to prove oneself to authority figures through physical means. These natives want to be respected for their strength, power and courage. They work hard and are persistent in their efforts but often are taken for granted by the very authority figures from whom they seek acknowledgment. They often must take initiatives on their own, for they get no support from the superiors whose business it is to assist them. Many natives develop a rugged individualist philosophy that extols pulling oneself up by one's own bootstraps. This combination of factors invites manipulation, through challenge, into accepting difficult or unpleasant tasks. These people eventually avoid the trap of responding to dares when they accept human frailty.

The Mars-MC/IC inconjunct indicates problems related to power, authority and aggression. Many natives feel constrained by circumstances and have to defer to authority figures who demand submission. They champion the underdog and want to force authorities to change their ways of acting. Other natives ambitiously pursue career success and social status. There is leadership ability but these types must learn to let things pass, for they can become tyrants. They do not tolerate opposition and may abuse the people under them. These natives can be either dictators or rebels. When they play dictator, they arouse rebellious opposition in others. When they play rebel, they either advocate force or pacifism to change society. These natives can be attracted to people with a messiah complex.

This aspect indicates career difficulties related to problems in self-assertion. These natives find it hard to assert their authority in an appropriate manner. They seem to need permission to act or assert themselves. Inability to take initiative often undermines their position. Hypocritical peacefulness prevents revealing anger in public. Some natives attain release by venting frustration against their own families. Other natives repress their anger and become passive aggressive. Both types are forced to control anger and restrain impulsiveness in career situations, for hasty action compromises career position. These people often are faced with a choice between spending time and energy with family, at home, or neglecting family in pursuit of career advancement. Either path seems to lead to disappointment, for they eventually come to miss the neglected avenue and seek to reclaim it later in life.

These natives have the virtue of working hard to further their careers. This inconjunct can indicate a strong and daring nature suitable for athletics, police work, the military or executive leadership. These people may find satisfaction as a lawyer, policeman, army general, surgeon, mediator, enforcer or bouncer. They may advocate confrontation as the means to change society. After becoming disillusioned, they may retreat to the privacy of their family and put their energies into tending their own garden.

JUPITER INCONJUNCT SATURN

The theme here is prudence. These natives are learning to assess situations realistically, perfect management skills and allow opportunities to develop. They are challenged to stop trying to impress people, overcome pessimism and develop a sense of humor.

This aspect indicates a sensitive and discriminating nature. These natives have a serious demeanor and a conservative philosophy. They have problems understanding when to be generous and when to be frugal. They eventually develop respect for realism and balance. They learn to weigh opportunities carefully and test the water before taking the plunge. They learn to control the gambling instinct and become accomplished in combative situations. Their thirst for experience and knowledge requires patience to assure success. They come into their own late in life.

The Jupiter-Saturn inconjunct indicates a desire to make a mature and responsible impression. These natives want to be respected, especially by authorities. They want acknowledgment for their maturity and responsibility from important people. The need to make an imposing impression may lead them to exaggerate their own authority. Their refusal to risk compromise of dignity may lead to pompousness. They use generosity to purchase respect, and are helpful to people with burdens, especially financial ones. They feel oppressed by others' expectations. They do favors for people who don't respect them, and sometimes lose respect by making promises they cannot fulfill.

There may be an inability to take advantage of opportunities due to poor timing or lack of perspective. These natives can be falsely optimistic or needlessly pessimistic. Lack of sociability or fear of competition creates problems. Lack of perspective can make them rigid, unspontaneous or legalistic . These people tend to underrate themselves and misjudge their opportunities. Sometimes, however, it is other people who underestimate their experience or ability to handle responsibility. These natives may miss out on opportunities due to inexperience or bad timing. They expand when they should withdraw, or retreat when they should advance. They must learn to wait for opportunities to develop. They must also learn to manage resources more realistically, for swings between frugality and excess make them penny-wise and pound-foolish.

This aspect indicates problems in relationships due to defensiveness and self-limitation. These people can't seem to get close to others because they fear restriction and loss of freedom. Fear of criticism leads them to be critical, and fear of abandonment makes them avoid closeness. Lack of faith makes it hard for them to compete socially. Time and distance seem to intrude in their relationships. Responsibility and lack of time are the excuses by which they avoid intimacy. Sometimes, however, they avoid intimacy by relating to people who are too busy or too distant to be close. They must learn to loosen up and take themselves less seriously, for their inability to take a joke is another factor which hampers relationship.

This inconjunct ultimately develops business acumen based upon patience, practicality and realistic assessment. These natives eventually become skilled at management and administration. They learn to evaluate people, money and resources realistically. An ability to temper risk with caution makes them good executives. They also may be excellent teachers, especially if they can learn to take themselves less seriously, accept limitations and see the humor in life.

JUPITER INCONJUNCT URANUS

The theme here is rugged individualism. These natives are learning to encourage individualism, create new opportunities and provoke the reassessment of basic assumptions. They are challenged to stop trying to impress others, develop close personal relationships and overcome the impulse to be disruptive.

These natives believe in fair play and equal opportunity, and want people to be free and independent. They think for themselves and see the world from a different perspective. Their unique approach to problems yields original ideas which may be turned to profit. They can be impulsively expansive and show generosity by surprising people with sudden gifts or big gestures.

This inconjunct may indicate a powerful need to make a shocking or upsetting impression. These natives can be rebellious or iconoclastic. They may have an independent philosophy or a unique moral code. While unusual subjects interest them, they attract friends who belittle new ideas or concepts. They like to play devil's advocate and delight in puncturing the arguments of the orthodox. Their thinking represents a search for truth at the root level. They threaten others because they seek to tear down facades, and pay the price of derision and attack.

The Jupiter-Uranus inconjunct indicates a battle between conformity and independence. These natives have a strong sense of individualism and independence but feel pressured to conform to avoid competitive disadvantage. Other people frequently misjudge them, exaggerate their eccentricities and deny them opportunities. They also lose opportunities through their own rebellious and inconsistent behavior. These people use their money to support rebellious or independent projects, and may waste money in support of an exaggeratedly individualistic life style. They are ultimately forced to curb their excesses or risk loss of independence. These people feel overwhelmed by the expectations of others and may fail in order to defeat this pressure. They also need to be careful not to compromise their independence through excessive generosity. Many types yield to social pressure and develop conventional life styles, becoming conservative but still attracting rebellious, inconsistent or eccentric people. They have to manage things for erratic or undisciplined people and wind up being conservative anomalies. This makes them stand out as nonconformists.

This aspect indicates difficulties in relationship due to fear of attachment. A strong independent streak makes it difficult for these natives to cooperate in relationships. The need for freedom and nonattachment makes intimacy difficult. They worry about being abandoned suddenly but can, themselves, suddenly abandon people or projects. They think abstractly, but impersonally, and find it hard to be empathic. These natives relate to people in a cold, impersonal way and are reluctant to reveal the softer side of their natures. An involvement with those who live at a distance precludes the possibility of intimacy. Erratic and irresponsible behavior is another impediment to closeness. They wind up relating to others through the mind rather than through the body, and develop intellectual relationships.

This inconjunct is useful for people who must think independently or work with extremely independent people. It might be applicable in creative management and the administration of unusual projects. The aspect can be useful for producers who must work with creative but unreliable people. These natives might become designers who develop novel approaches. They might utilize their desire to defend unpopular causes in the service of law and become excellent lawyers.

JUPITER INCONJUNCT NEPTUNE

The theme here is social conscience. These natives are learning to accept obligations, fulfill commitments and evaluate creative inspiration. They are challenged to develop faith, avoid ambivalence and overcome escapist tendencies.

These natives have a generous, sympathetic and encouraging nature. Their philosophical leanings and a strong moral code emphasizes fulfillment of commitments. They can be generous in support of religious or spiritual causes. This type can also be attracted by the glamour of status or may seek to create impressive images.

This aspect indicates problems related to confusion and escapism. These natives can be overconcerned with image and facade. They may indulge in fantasies of success but lack faith in their own resources. They are beset by ambivalence and self-doubt. A need for reassurance eventually causes others to doubt their capabilities. These types can sometimes be gullible, indulging in wishful thinking, daydreams or fantasies. Realistic assessment, therefore, has little chance against self-delusion. They sometimes can tell exaggerated stories or confuse people with contradictory statements. Vagueness and inattention can be used as a strategy to avoid commitments. Some natives waste money and resources on escapist pursuits or on drugs. Most, however, try hard to be practical and make realistic assessment of circumstances their goal, for they realize that uncertainty, self-doubt and vacillation are their chief obstacles to success.

The Jupiter-Neptune inconjunct indicates problems related to fulfillment of commitments. These natives express generosity by accepting obligations, making promises they cannot fulfill. They may commit to projects and then lose interest. They may feel obliged to live up to others' expectations. People take their generosity for granted and commit them to financial obligations. Some natives learn to avoid commitments and collect debts, instead, by voluntarily doing favors. They master the politics of guilt and learn how to make people feel obligated.

There may be difficulties related to lack of perspective and bad judgment. These people tend to misjudge themselves and others. They send and receive double messages and misread other people's intentions.

Their relationships too often are based upon misunderstandings. They may attract confused or disorganized people whom they have to assist. They misjudge their own importance, either by overestimating or belittling themselves. Lack of confidence turns out to be self-destructive because they jeopardize opportunities through ambivalence or vacillation. They frequently fail to recognize opportunities at hand. They tend to place their faith unwisely in others. Romantic idealism precludes a realistic assessment of partners, and an excessive need for freedom makes it difficult to get close to others. These natives seem to attract fickle or escapist partners who abandon them in time of need. They must learn to see others as they are and accept them for what they are.

This inconjunct develops an ability to work with and organize creative projects. These natives may become accomplished at managing creative projects. The aspect may be useful in commercial art or advertising. These natives may excel as art directors or producers. Other vocational possibilities for this aspect include philosophy, law, religion, fund raising or promotion.

JUPITER INCONJUNCT PLUTO

The theme here is analytical perspective. These natives are learning to analyze potential, see things in perspective and take advantage of uncertainty. They are challenged to overcome obsessiveness, forego dogmatic attitudes and stop trying to impress people.

This aspect indicates an expansive and encouraging disposition. These natives have a generous nature which induces them to help others. Their inability to say no, however, encourages people to seek favors. These types possess a strong urge for freedom which makes them resist being pigeonholed. They have excellent analytical minds and a talent for research and analysis.

There may be a powerful need to impress people. These natives tend to be overconcerned with the good opinion of others. A need to be treated with dignity causes them to be upright, but this sometimes degenerates into self-righteous pomposity. These types eventually learn to create an impressive facade. Their social ability is directly related to their financial stability. Money, therefore, becomes the key to social success. They either live well below their means, in a sort of voluntary poverty, or well beyond their means. Both types tend to cling to privileges, which turn out to be disadvantages. Many of these natives suffer from poor social perspective.

Inability to assess themselves and others causes them to misjudge people. Fear of being underrated by others sometimes causes them to boast or exaggerate. Lack of faith in their own resources causes them to unnecessarily issue disclaimers. These people have a strong drive for success, but a fear of failure keeps them from taking the risks that lead to success. They must learn to take advantage of opportunities as they present themselves, but, in order to do this, they must forego the need for guarantees and the desire to maintain dignity at all costs.

The Jupiter-Pluto inconjunct indicates a rigid and dogmatic nature, which betrays a fear of uncertainty. These natives can be obsessive and unspontaneous. The need for certainty causes them to try to live by agendas. An inability to adjust to new circumstances makes it difficult for them to take advantage of unexpected opportunities. These people can be legalistic, dogmatic or orthodox. A conservative nature induces them to cling to the past. A tendency to substitute philosophy for life experience impedes their ability to learn and grow. Some natives develop a doctrinaire philosophical attitude which cannot tolerate opposition. Other natives take it upon themselves to challenge or reform dogma. Both types eventually learn to integrate new experience with tried and proven ways, and come to accept their vulnerability in a world of uncertainty and change.

This aspect indicates difficulty in developing intimate relationships. These natives have strong escapist tendencies when it comes to emotional commitment. The need for elbow room, and fear of attachment, makes them retreat when others approach. They have poor judgment when selecting potential partners, and are often attracted to people who either are indisposed or unavailable for relationship. They forsake opportunities for involvement and abandon potential partners before giving them a chance. These types also involve themselves with people who abandon them without warning. Inability to tolerate uncertainty makes them interrogate people about every aspect of their lives, which ultimately oppresses and drives others away.

This inconjunct develops analytical management ability, which might be useful in supervisory positions. These natives might excel at sales, advertising or diplomacy. Other vocational avenues include teaching, psychology, acting or investment analysis.

JUPITER INCONJUNCT ASC/DSC

The focus here is personality. These natives are learning to manage money, evaluate people realistically and help others with their tasks. They are challenged to develop intimate relationships and stop trying to buy or impress people.

This aspect indicates a generous, optimistic and encouraging nature. These natives are ethical and possess a strong moral code. They love to travel and have an exaggerated need for freedom. Their interest in philosophy and metaphysics leads to the development and sharing of knowledge. They tend to be interested in the broad scope and have little patience for detail. Generalities rather than specifics are of concern to them. Attainment of wisdom and living according to one's beliefs eventually come to be the goals which define their lives.

The Jupiter-ASC/DSC inconjunct indicates personality excesses related to a need to impress people with their importance. A need to carry themselves with dignity makes these natives very upright. A need for dignity causes them to appear sanctimonious, moralistic, self-righteous or pompous. Some types develop over-expansive personalities. They may be opportunistic, boastful, grandiose or blustering to emphasize a need to be important. Other natives quietly play the role of manager or philosopher and attract people who constantly need their assistance. They are taken advantage of until they understand the underlying causes.

There may be a tendency to misjudge people and circumstances. These natives seem to consistently underestimate or overrate others. They are generous to the wrong people and misjudge partners or competitors. They also are attracted to people who belittle them. It is not unusual for them to self-destructively help competitors. They lack the killer instinct and unwisely give enemies a second chance. An inability to recognize an advantage causes them to waste opportunities, and the tendency to misjudge business opportunities leads them to invest unwisely. Lack of patience leads to the abandonment of projects prematurely. These people become adept at evaluation when they develop the patience to examine and integrate details into a broad perspective is developed.

This aspect indicates problems in achieving intimacy. These natives have an excessive need for freedom and feel crowded, confined or even smothered in close relationships. They hate to be pigeonholed and feel pressured by other people's expectations. They seem to be caught between the fear of attachment and the fear of abandonment. The simplest solution can sometimes be avoidance of intimacy. One good way of achieving this is to become involved with someone in a distant town. This has the advantage of allowing them to deceive themselves into thinking that they really want close relationships but the unlucky circumstance of long-distance separation prevents it. Many natives seek vicarious satisfaction through relationship and have expectations that no partner can meet. However, they often attract people who use them as a screen for their projections. Some natives either waste their partner's money or attract partners who waste their money. Money matters, therefore, become a divisive issue in relationships. Some natives see marriage as a means of enhancing their social standing; these marriages may become more of a business partnership than a loving relationship.

This inconjunct ultimately influences these people to become philosophical about life. They tend to be late bloomers who grow happier and more fulfilled as they grow older. This aspect can be very useful in teaching, money management, advertising or promotion. When these natives learn to assess people accurately, they make excellent managers.

JUPITER INCONJUNCT MC/IC

This aspect indicates a concern with education and knowledge as the key to achievement. These natives have a philosophical nature and broad metaphysical interests. An expansive and generous disposition urges them to social participation. A philanthropic nature interests them in the plight of the disadvantaged. Many take pride in, and rarely stray from their roots. They feel comfortable around home and family. Quality of home life becomes the key to their personal fulfillment, and they lavish their love and pride upon family. Other natives, with a more cosmopolitan nature, become intellectual explorers who expose themselves to new ideas and come to break the bounds of cultural limitation.

The Jupiter-MC/IC inconjunct indicates an inordinate need for power and prestige. These natives want to play an important social role, either for recognition or social standing. The tendency to view society in terms of class distinctions induces them to seek privilege. A distaste for subordinate roles makes them difficult employees. They are much happier in supervisory positions, because this satisfies their desire for status. Ambition becomes a force in their lives and they eventually aspire to impressive jobs or careers which offer dignity or prestige, if not financial reward. These natives can be opinionated and outspoken. They either are freethinkers or orthodox and legalistic. The former are caught in the bind of ambivalent rebelliousness. They want to speak out but also want permission to do so. And, they resent those who grant them permission. These natives are usually forced to contend with rigidly conservative authority. The more orthodox types tend to become pompous, self-righteous or sanctimonious, resisting new ideas and resenting liberal thinking. Their views stunt intellectual development and make it difficult for them to adjust to change.

There may be a conflict between home life and a desire for achievement. These natives often have to choose between dedication to career or devotion to family. Either choice leaves a sense of unfulfillment and resentment in the sacrifice of the other. Those who dedicate themselves to career find that professional demands cause the neglect of family and public achievement compromises privacy. Those who devote themselves to home and family find career development compromised. The more immature of these natives come to blame and resent family for their lack of professional advancement. This attitude makes them poor parents. These natives might project their own ambitions onto their children and burden them with impossible expectations. They either overestimate their children or belittle them for lack of achievement. They may, in turn, be secretly belittled and eventually abandoned as the children grow up and pursue their own interests.

This aspect indicates career difficulties related to poor judgment and lack of perspective. These natives tend to exaggerate their own importance and misjudge the people who work for them. The tendency to underestimate and belittle subordinates drives away talented people and leaves them with mediocrity. Their lack of support or encouragement breeds discontent and resentment. These natives also have difficulty perceiving potential. Their overenthusiasm dies quickly with the first problems, causing them to abandon projects without allowing them sufficient time to develop. A tendency to overmanage things ultimately leads to failure. It would be wise for them to allow talented subordinates the freedom to work, for once these natives become involved, they mismanage and blow things out of proportion.

This inconjunct ultimately teaches the art of realistic assessment. This, combined with the need for social standing, eventually makes these natives good supervisors, managers or administrators. Other vocational possibilities include financial management, securities investment, fund raising or banking. These natives may also excel in advertising, publishing or travel. An interest in philosophy, knowledge and the sharing of information might lead them to become teachers, historians or writers.

SATURN INCONJUNCT URANUS

The theme here is freedom v. responsibility. These natives are learning to confront authority, overcome restrictive tradition and take the time to effect change. They are challenged to accept responsibility, curb impulsiveness and participate socially.

This aspect indicates a highly individualistic nature, with a talent for developing original structures. These natives tend to have logical minds and a good ability to solve problems. They have an outsider's perspective and a different point of view, which makes them an enigma to others. The ability to think deeply and thoroughly allows them to uncover root causes. Their conservative approach to unusual subjects borders on the scientific. They have an urge to turn things upside down, but a sense of responsibility makes them favor evolution over revolution. These natives may have friends but tend to be loners and nonparticipants in some major area of life. They need time and solitude to sort things through. They thoroughly consider options and then make impulsive decisions. After interminable hesitation, these types act to make changes swiftly, suddenly and radically.

The Saturn-Uranus inconjunct indicates a conflict between freedom and responsibility. These natives feel conflicted about accepting responsibility because they fear that it might compromise their independence. They are proud of their individuality and take pains to assert their nonconformist nature. They respect other people's eccentricities and want the same respect for their own. Many of these natives feel isolated and separ-ated from the mainstream. Their differences make them feel restricted, and they tend to avoid participation in competitive activities. Impulsive and undisciplined at first, they learn through life circumstances that the development of patience and self-discipline is necessary to achieve social success. Experience also teaches them that permanence requires patience, budgeting is essential to independence, and freedom comes from self-discipline. They become the voice of realism among the impulsive, undisciplined and rebellious, but must be careful to avoid discouraging people through pessimistic or restrictive attitudes. In time they learn to balance the considerations of freedom v. responsibility and individuality v. conformity, and become valuable members of society.

There may be an overconcern with perfection. These natives are very tough on themselves. They judge themselves by severe standards of excellence and demand perfection. Their desire to be unique makes them dissatisfied with mere competence. Perfection, however, demands self–discipline, an attribute these natives lack. The perfectionistic tendency also manifests in their relationships. Their attraction to people is often based upon ideals of perfection that no one can meet. They place others upon pedestals, but their gods are merely mortal and are bound, sooner or later, to show human frailty. When this happens, they lose interest and pursue other screens for the projection of their ideals. This mechanism creates personal anxiety and barriers to relationship as long as it continues. They must eventually come to accept their ordinariness, join the rest of the human race and enjoy the company of flawed, fellow mortals.

This aspect indicates problems related to rebellion against authority. These natives see themselves as individualists struggling against oppressive tradition. They feel pressured to conform by a society that resists change. Some natives rebel by being erratic or unreliable. Other types express themselves by iconoclastically attacking the very foundations of the established order. Their rebellious nature delights in upsetting conservatives by expressing the most shocking ideas or sentiments. They serve society in the process, however, by forcing the reassessment of accustomed beliefs.

This inconjunct imparts a need to break with the norm, which permits these natives to pursue unusual interests such as astrology or other occult/metaphysical subjects. The desire to be innovative may be turned to creative design or invention. These people also might be attracted to nontraditional vocations. Their logical/rational faculties suggest writing or problem solving.

SATURN INCONJUNCT NEPTUNE

The theme here is illusion v. reality. These natives are learning to fulfill obligations, accept responsibility and structure creative efforts. They are challenged to resist unfair burdens, overcome self-doubt and stop setting impossible goals.

This aspect indicates a potential for giving form to dreams and vague sensations. These natives have a practical imagination and an ability to create inspiring images, which aids them in creative endeavors. Their religious or philosophical views tend to have a scientific orientation. A skeptical nature makes them test new intuitions against the reality of everyday existence and helps in the selection of the most practical ideas.

These natives are realistic and responsible or inspired but impractical. Unless they discipline themselves, their overindulgent imaginations compromise their sense of reality. Daydreaming takes the place of productive activity, causing mistakes and wasting time. Fantasy becomes the escape from reality, and unattended responsibilities create burdens for others. Ambivalence and indecisiveness create additional problems for them. Uncertainty causes vacillating attitudes and confused communication. Mixed messages and double meanings seem to plague relationships. They must, therefore, take the time, to be sure that they know what they want and say what they feel. They must also be sure they understand what other people actually mean. Many natives maintain unrealistic ideals and standards of perfection. Double standards may sometimes be at issue as well. They eventually learn that definiteness and consistency are the virtues which they need in order to control the chaos in their lives.

There may be a tendency to suffer from fear and doubt. These natives worry over intangibles and develop self-limiting fears or fantasies. Anxiety and self-doubt makes them seek reassurance from others, but this has the unintended effect of inducing others to doubt them as well. They worry about their competence and their inexperience. Unfounded fears keep them isolated and discourage participation or competition. Their pessimism discourages creative activity and caution leads to ambivalence and hesitation. These types overcome their problems once they learn that the real is rarely as fearful as the imagined. In order to learn this, they must take risks in spite of their doubts and fears.

This inconjunct indicates problems related to acceptance of burdens and responsibilities. These natives tend to see themselves as saints or martyrs who are obliged to accept other people's burdens. Their inability to resist unfair obligations is based upon a need to win other people's respect for their maturity and sense of responsibility. These people feel obliged to defer to elders or authority, and support tradition. They also accept the burden of creating order out of chaos and disciplining confused or impractical people. They get pressured into donating their free time and get too caught up in responsibilities to take a vacation. Drugs, alcohol or illness may, therefore, become escape routes for the release of burdens. These natives must be patient with others and learn when not to interfere even though others are making mistakes. This bears fruit because people learn from their mistakes and develop the skills which allow them to relieve future burdens for these individuals.

This inconjunct might be useful in both fine and commercial arts. This planetary combination also suggests theater, photography, dance, writing or poetry as fruitful outlets. If used well, it might be one indicator of musical talent.

SATURN INCONJUNCT PLUTO

The theme here is overcoming fixation. These natives are learning to accept responsibility, relax rigid standards and share responsibilities. They are challenged to overcome obsessive pessimism, forego the need to control, and put aside doctrinaire tradition.

This aspect indicates a serious mind with a strong sense of reality. It gives a scientific mind and good analytical ability. These natives can be cautious and circumspect. Their skeptical nature requires time in order to accept new ideas. They can be discerning and discriminating. Their sensitive nature demands the highest quality. They settle for nothing less than excellence and work hard to achieve it.

There may be an obsessive need for control. Many of these natives are drawn to the security of rigid structure. This tendency sometimes attracts them to authority figures to whom they must surrender their personal power. They develop a symbiotic relationship which permits their own power needs to be satisfied vicariously. Sooner or later, however, they either get a taste of power or experience the unpleasantness of impotence. This becomes the stimulus to develop their own inner authority. Once they decide to assert their power, they come face to face with oppressive tradition which forbids it. They must, therefore, develop patience and learn the art of diplomacy. In some natives, the obsessive need for control manifests as a mania for neatness or cleanliness. Promptness becomes a prime virtue and frugality a way of life. These people can't stand delay, but they may make use of stalling tactics to assert their power. They have to be careful, for their pessimistic and overcontrolling nature oppresses others. It would be wise for them to practice letting go of control by delegating their authority.

The Saturn-Pluto inconjunct indicates a great need for certainty. These natives live with a "what if" obsession that makes them fear the future. The tendency to cling to agendas precludes spontaneity. Inability to adjust makes them rigid and doctrinaire. Many of these people need guidelines and boundaries to make them feel comfortable. They want standards by which to measure themselves, even if the standards are inappropriate. This creates major problems in relationship. Fear of uncertainty makes these types oppressively prying. Separation anxiety leads them to become clinging or dependent. Both tendencies ultimately have the reverse effect of driving away others.

This aspect indicates a need to prove one's maturity to others. These natives can be sober, reserved, cautious, conservative and traditional. They want to prove themselves realistic, reliable and responsible. The need to be respected and taken seriously permits others to withhold acknowledgment as a manipulative ploy. These natives may, therefore, be maneuvered into giving up time or accepting unwanted responsibilities. They may even be manipulated into accepting responsibility without the power or authority that ought to accompany it. These people are often burdened by a lack of funding to fulfill their tasks. This eventually forces them to learn the art of budgeting and effective money management. In the process, they also learn to marshal their resources and become efficient managers.

This inconjunct indicates a potential talent for structural analysis, which can be useful in design or engineering. It may also be successfully employed in scientific pursuits, research, computer programming or psychology. The ability to think analytically and comprehend motivation may also be applied in the theater or in sales.

SATURN INCONJUNCT ASC/DSC

The theme here is responsibility. These natives are learning to be patient, accept responsibility and take others seriously. They are challenged to overcome pessimism, stop discouraging others and participate in social activities.

This aspect indicates a serious, reserved demeanor. These natives are rational/skeptical types with a conservative/traditional philosophy. They can be very sensitive, perceptive or discriminating. The tendency to take life seriously, perhaps too seriously, takes the fun out of living. In time they may lighten up, see the humor in life and learn to laugh at their own foibles.

The Saturn–ASC/DSC inconjunct indicates an excessive need to be mature and responsible. These natives want respect and are willing to work for it. High standards of quality make them discriminating and demanding. Discipline and hard work become the assets that help them overcome inexperience. They want to be realistic and try to be economical. They budget resources carefully, but a bias toward frugality often nakes them impractical. Many of these natives are forced by circumstances to accept burdens or take responsibility for others. They may attract immature or unrealistic people who waste their time and resources. They may be harried by lack of time to perform their duties. Some natives are forced to confront rigid authorities or outmoded traditions. An inner sense of responsibility makes it impossible to let things go and forces them to accept the full burden of long-overdue change.

This aspect indicates a tendency to develop a rigid personality. Tradition is important to these natives, but it often serves to inhibit self-development. The tendency to adopt severe and uncompromising standards makes flexibility difficult. A crusty facade and pessimistic ways tend to discourage others from approaching. Lack of experience makes them stilted in relationships. They, therefore, may keep too much to themselves and feel lonely or isolated. Their social awkwardness makes it hard for them to participate or compete. Their distant manner creates an authority figure which invites deference rather than friendship. A methodical nature precludes spontaneity and attracts rigid people, and it doesn't help one enjoy life. These natives eventually come to value flexibility as a major step toward fulfillment.

There may be difficulty in relationship due to perfectionistism. These natives must learn to be less intolerant and more patient with potential partners, for a fussy and critical nature prevents fulfillment of relationship needs. They want a serious involvement but defensiveness creates barriers to closeness. Many of these natives either seek parent surrogates or play the parent role themselves. They don't like to be kept waiting, but partnerships demand patience, for it takes a lot of time to build trust. The tendency to seek difficulty attracts them to immature, cautious or defensive people who require much wooing. These relationships may be more burdensome than pleasurable, but they seem to fulfill an inner attraction to hardship. Frugality and other money issues strain their unions sooner or later. Development of patience and understanding becomes the mortar which keeps their relationships intact.

This aspect indicates a talent for leadership and sound management, provided that these natives learn to accept other people's imperfections. This aspect indicates vocational potential in accounting, banking or money management. The ability to organize and convey information with authority can make for excellent teaching ability. These natives also may find success in engineering, the sciences, anthropology, commercial art, music, dance or other pursuits where attention to detail, disciplined effort and repetition bear fruit.

SATURN INCONJUNCT MC/IC

The theme here is authority. These natives are learning to assert their authority, demand respect and accept social responsibility. They are challenged to forego resentment, develop patience and stop looking for recognition from authorities.

This aspect indicates a serious, sensitive and discriminating nature with a feeling for structure and control. These people can be realistic but pessimistic. A need for privacy and solitude tends to separate them from others. They can be cautious or guarded, but when they speak, they seem to carry a natural authority. Career/family issues come to dominate their concerns. They must eventually choose between either separation from family in order to further personal development, or devotion to family and the subversion of personal growth.

There may be a tendency to be burdened by one's family. These natives tend to be taken advantage of by family members who unload burdens and responsibilities on their doorstep. They are often forced to be mature while others are irresponsible or childlike. There may be a vulnerability to parental accusations of immaturity or irresponsibility. They want respect from parents or family but these natives are merely taken for granted. They can be economical and conservative. Their frugality may be self-imposed or the consequence of real life hardships. They seek acknowledgement from people who withhold it, and find it difficult to be playful and care-free. They can feel hindered in their aspirations and compelled to wait for career opportunities. Circumstances and personal burdens make them feel isolated or lonely, and they may take out frustrations on family members. They eventually learn that disregard of family pressure is the only way to lighten up and begin to live one's own life. The first, most important and most difficult, step in this process is physical and emotional self-exile from family members.

The Saturn–MC/IC inconjunct indicates a desire for respect and authority through worldly achievement. These natives have a powerful need to win the acknowledgment of authority figures and to become authorities themselves. They try hard to prove themselves reliable and responsible but fall short of the mark because they lack patience and self-discipline. Their careers develop slowly, but in the end they achieve the authoritative position they seek. These individuals have to be careful not to mistake pessimism for realism, because they can easily discourage others. They may be required to contend with discouraging authorities who have their eyes firmly fixed on the past. They may be forced to chal-lenge tradition and experience persecution for new ideas, inexperience or youthfulness. People in authority tend to be overly severe toward them. These natives may also be severe and stern when given authority. There is a strong tendency toward arrogance, which comes out when they feel superior. If they are lucky, success will be delayed until they learn to temper their arrogance with humility.

This inconjunct indicates a natural managerial ability that makes these natives good executives or administrators. A sense of economy and the desire to control the use of resources may lend itself to economics or accounting. These people also carry a natural authority which makes them suitable as teachers.

URANUS INCONJUNCT NEPTUNE

The issue here might be individuality and independence v. obligation, anxiety in the face of confusion or anxiety resulting from vague fears and delusions. This person may wish to shock people out of their illusions. He might compromise independence through vagueness, vacillation and uncertainty, and tend to undermine himself through erraticness or eccentricity. This may also indicate a person who is creative or inventive. However, this aspect is a generational one, and will affect many people born at a particular time.

URANUS INCONJUNCT PLUTO

The issues here might be obsession with differences, anxiety in the face of uncertainty or loss of control. This person might be nonconformist, individualistic or rebellious. He might be tense and anxious. There may be a compulsion to upset others, and to become obsessed with doing one's own thing. This aspect may lead one to instigate rebellion or manipulate others by playing upon their anxieties. The individual may be erratic, or may feel pressured to get rid of eccentricities. This aspect may indicate the beginning of a new revolutionary doctrine. Because it, too, will affect a generation, it must be interpreted in terms of a group rather than on a highly individual basis.

URANUS INCONJUNCT ASC/DSC

The theme here is nonconformity. These natives are learning to be independent, develop an individual style and accept other people's eccentricities. They are challenged to be more reliable, stop provoking people and develop closer ties.

This aspect indicates a creative, original, impulsive nature. These natives can be intellectually competitive and have excellent minds, especially for abstract concepts. They can be good at debugging, problem solving or unraveling riddles. A mild exterior hides deep passions. They tend to friendships and impersonal involvements rather than close, intimate relationships.

The Uranus-ASC/DSC inconjunct indicates a tendency to be contrary. These natives can be rebellious. Their eccentric or perverse nature attracts them to the unusual or bizarre. A desire to overturn things leads them to take opposing points of view. They love to play devil's advocate and upset people by challenging their beliefs on the most basic level. A delight in using shock tactics upsets others and creates a barrier to closeness and openness. These natives eventually learn the value of discipline, control their destructive urges and develop the ability to enlighten others without threatening them.

This aspect indicates difficulty in relationship due to an excessive need to be different. These natives have different ideas about relationship. Unusual values induce them to seek unusual partnerships. They may be attracted to experimental or role reversal relationships. Their independent urges jeopardize relationships and their impulsiveness ruins marriages. These individuals can be attracted to erratic or unreliable partners. Fear of losing individuality leads to too much mutual independence and a battle of wills. They tend to be emotionally inexpressive and anxiety laden. Their tendency to be impersonal rather than intimate makes friendship more attractive than marriage. These natives often have a strong affect on other people's relationships. They may have a tendency to disrupt partnerships or cooperative ventures.

These natives have a strong desire to assert their individuality. They can be rebellious, stubborn or willful. Some types have distinguishing physical characteristics that mark them. The desire to be unique may make them perfectionistic. Eccentricities and personal mannerisms lead others to see them as odd. Nonconformist tendencies lead to repressive social pressure. Natives who conform feel their individuality oppressed. Repressed rebelliousness leads them to frustrate others through erratic behavior, errors and delays. These natives may attract rebellious, eccentric people who cause them discomfort and difficulty.

This inconjunct indicates a natural sense of antagonism that might be useful in advocacy or contention. These natives may enjoy debate or law. An interest in abstract practicalities makes them good at problem solving. They can make good computer programmers if they develop some self-discipline. These natives also might become writers or creative artists. They also may be attracted by vocations that feature novelty or change.

URANUS INCONJUNCT MC/IC

The theme here is social rebellion. These natives are learning to stimulate people, confront authority and resist regimentation. They are challenged to forego resentment, moderate iconoclastic urges and overcome the temptation to provoke others.

This aspect indicates an independent and innovative nature. These natives tend to have a talent for abstract thinking and problem solving. They like to think for themselves and develop their own way of doing things. Their desire to break structures leads them to challenge traditional practices. The desire for innovation induces them to experiment with new methods. They are attracted to avant-garde systems and gravitate toward novelty and excitement. In their eagerness to effect change, they must take care to insure that they don't sacrifice effective practices before they validate new ones.

The Uranus-MC/IC inconjunct indicates a rebellious resistance to authority. These natives take pride in possessing rebellious or iconoclastic feelings. They can be rebels without a cause, but there is ambivalence there, for they want permission to rebel from the very authorities they oppose. Since permission is rarely given, they tend to feel frustrated and resentful. Some natives have shocking views that they wish to impose upon society. The desire to uproot and overturn convention upsets others, and creates even more social pressure on them to suppress their views. They may react by becoming resentful and impatient with people. The stronger their feelings, and the more self-indulgent their expression, the greater the resistance they generate in others. The only way out of this trap is to become more patient with others, develop an understanding of people's real concerns and learn to address others in nonthreatening ways.

There may be a conflict between individuality and the need for career or social achievement. These natives tend to think of themselves as special. They want to be different, but don't like the sacrifice this entails. They feel pressured to conceal their differences and eccentricities in order to avoid offending superiors. Conformity becomes a problem because it is often prerequisite to career advancement. They are, therefore, forced to control or inhibit individualistic urges, but the resulting erratic or inconsistent behavior forms another impediment to success. This creates a crisis which must be faced: Is career or social achievement worth the sacrifice of individuality?

This aspect indicates a need to resist oppressive family influences. These natives are made to feel different by family members who seem able to inhibit or stifle them. Their individuality and independence is compromised by parental demands for support. The resulting frustration and resentment, if unexpressed, either creates anxiety and all sorts of illness, or attracts violence. These natives suffer until they declare their independence from family pressures and expectations. Until then, they tend to take frustrations out on themselves and their children. The irony here is that they want to make their home a very special place. They can achieve this aim only when they realize that their life is their life and not their family's.

This inconjunct indicates a desire to confront society with the urgency for change. It is a good aspect for a researcher, reporter, writer or reformer. The interest in uncovering the hidden past might make for a good historian, archeologist or psychologist. These natives might be better off with their own business rather than working for others. The new or revolutionary might then further the career instead of hindering it.

NEPTUNE INCONJUNCT PLUTO

This aspect is too universal to give more than a few speculative thoughts. The energy might become individualized during a transit if it reinforces other characteristics of the natal chart.

Some possibilities for the combination:
obsession as a form of escape from reality
constant daydreaming
alcoholism or drug abuse
martyrdom
craftiness and deception
transformative visions
high inspiration and mysticism
religious longings, transcendent experiences
demanding an end to vagueness and double meanings
demand for clarity
very ethical – what "ought" to be

NEPTUNE INCONJUNCT ASC/DSC

The theme here is ambiguity. These natives are learning to make decisions, express themselves clearly and see people as they really are. They are challenged to stop vacillating, overcome self-doubt and stop being an escapist.

This aspect indicates creative inspiration. These natives have a good imagination. A talent for visualization allows them to inspire people through the use of imagery. They often have strong religious or mystical leanings, and take delight in art, music, dance or poetry. There is a natural charisma and an ability to influence people through suggestion. Good intuition and psychic sensitivity attune them to the nuances of people's feelings, and lets them make behavioral changes which disarm others.

The Neptune-ASC/DSC inconjunct indicates difficulty in developing relationships. These natives tend to harbor illusions about others. They have idealized concepts of behavior and unrealistic ideals about marriage. Their intensely romantic nature makes real relationships less attractive than fantasy ones. They tend to seek vicarious fulfillment through partnerships, and also serve as screens for other people's illusions. Unrealistic involvements lead to disillusionment. They need to learn that overly romantic notions preclude seeing situations realistically, and keeps them vulnerable to deception by insincere people. Ulterior motives create relationship problems. Many natives create problems through indecision, uncertainty and fickleness. Ambivalence creates double messages, engenders distrust and causes breakdown in communication. Financial obligation and waste of money becomes another divisive issue. These problems can be overcome through frankness and open negotiation.

This aspect indicates a strong fantasy life. These natives are more likely to be escapist than realistic. If they don't discipline themselves, daydreams may define their life style. Indulgence in fantasy becomes the major impediment to tackling life's problems, and procrastination takes the place of action. Inattention leads to confusion and costly errors. Preoccupation, absentmindedness and poor memory tend to offend others because they assume the natives are indifferent to them. Some natives turn to drugs or alcohol as an escape from the pressures of life. However, a lack of moderation may make them hypersensitive to drugs or stimulants.

There may be difficulty in making and sticking to decisions. These natives can be uncertain and indecisive. They seem unable to concentrate upon details and lack the discipline to complete projects. Their tendency to vacillate annoys and frustrates people. These individuals worry too much about inconsequentials and dwell upon what they ought to do. After a while, they may lose the capacity to determine what they really want. They can't seem to resist obligations because they find it difficult to say NO. They find it hard to shed unwanted obligations and usually fulfill commitments regardless of the personal cost to themselves. Redundancy is a special problem for them, for they repeat themselves differently each time. They eventually learn that simplicity and straightforwardness are the only antidotes to the disorder that complexity breeds.

This inconjunct indicates a subtle and creative mind suitable for art, music, poetry or writing. Religious feelings may find fulfillment through metaphysical studies. The ability to grow through meditation opens these types to the spiritual dimensions of life. Sensitivity to others gives them potential for psychic work. They also possess a natural gift for imagery that may find application in photography or advertising.

NEPTUNE INCONJUNCT MC/IC

The theme here is social obligation. These natives are learning to accept obligations, live up to commitments and inspire others. They are challenged to overcome self-doubt, forego resentment and stop vacillating.

This aspect indicates a highly imaginative nature. These natives have a talent for creative imagery and can be inspired. They may develop an interest in art, music or theater. Mystical leanings may attract them to philosophical or metaphysical pursuits. Some natives may develop deep religious or spiritual values that they share with people, while other natives inspire people through personal example.

The Neptune-MC/IC inconjunct indicates problems with authority related to confusion and self-doubt. These natives may resent authority, but also want acknowledgment from authority figures. Ambivalence attracts them to uncertain or chaotic situations. Superiors seem trapped in a morass of confusion. Indecision causes vacillation and makes achievement difficult. Self-doubts and a need for reassurance undermine their authority and encourage attempts to destroy whatever confidence they have. Unexpressed intentions and ulterior motives also create problems. Confused messages and double meanings impede communication. These natives eventually learn to approach authorities with clear intentions and simple, direct communication. This is especially important when they are in positions of authority, for ambivalence and lack of clarity engenders misconceptions and resentment in subordinates.

These natives harbor unrealistic beliefs about society and the world. They want the world to be a better place than it really is. They either see life through rose-colored glasses or in a cynical, disillusioned manner. The latter types tend to be very resentful. Many of these natives have a strong fantasy life, which leads them to daydream or dwell upon power. Unrealistic visions and escapist tendencies divert them from setting practical goals. Naive acceptance leads to deception and disillusionment. Life circumstances eventually lead them to become highly skeptical. They develop a pragmatic and realistic approach to life's problems. They have to be careful, however, to avoid attracting people, especially family members, who burden them with unwanted obligations. The simplest way of discouraging this is by saying NO, without explanation or justification.

This inconjunct develops aesthetic sensibilities that might be employed in creative endeavors. These natives may find fulfillment through art, music, photography or theater. They may be attracted by glamour careers. Their image-making ability might be well utilized in advertising or the media. They can be good in support or staff positions where they might explore new ideas without the inhibition of immediate practicality.

PLUTO INCONJUNCT ASC/DSC

The theme here is overcoming obsessions. These natives are learning to accept uncertainty, live with imperfection and let go of old relationships. They are challenged to overcome obsessiveness, forego dogmatic inclinations and stop trying to change people.

This aspect indicates a forceful and persistent nature. These natives can be determined and persevering once they set their minds on something. Their penetrating analytical minds enjoy research and investigative endeavors, but they must be careful to avoid getting bogged down in detail. The ability to appreciate psychological motivation adds depth to their relationships and helps others make the changes that enhance the quality of life.

The Pluto-ASC/DSC inconjunct indicates an obsessive personality. These natives can be unspontaneous, stilted or controlled. Their tendency to hold onto old memories, ideas or feelings creates a resistant and stagnant personality. A distaste for uncertainty makes them want to know all the details before they risk change. Their desire to apply rigid agendas proves fruitless since circumstances rarely work out as anticipated. A desire to be completely understood makes them repeat themselves redundantly, and exasperates or offends others. They can be redundant in many other ways as well. Most natives either are obsessively neat or very sloppy. The former can't seem to stand any type of disarray. A desire to clean things up or attain closure makes them dredge up old issues. The sloppy types tend to create disorder and confusion wherever they go. These natives eventually must learn to leave issues pending and accept things as they are. They must learn to accept being only 95% understood or, God forbid, only 75% understood. If they can do this, and also drop their agendas, they can experience renewal by living in the present.

There often are power struggles in relationship. These natives create their own problems by trying to control or manipulate partners. Their inability to tolerate uncertainty creates possessiveness. These natives either obsess about partners or attract obsessive and manipulative partners who try to change them. Money, children and control are major divisive issues in their relationships, especially control of children or finances. Rigid feelings and doctrinaire attitudes create resistance to change and unwillingness to cooperate. Dogmatic beliefs create barriers between themselves and others. These natives must learn, therefore, to put aside their biases and accept people for what they are instead of trying to reform them.

This inconjunct helps one develop persistence and analytical skill. These natives may make good researchers, investigators or analysts. An interest in motivation can make them successful at psychology, sales or acting. These individuals also might make good stock market analysts.

PLUTO INCONJUNCT MC/IC

The theme here is power. These natives are learning to develop political acumen, delegate power and initiate change. They are challenged to overcome obsessiveness, forego resentment and avoid coerciveness.

This aspect indicates a persevering nature. These natives have a powerful drive for accomplishment. Dedication and hard work give them the ability to finish difficult tasks. They can be tactful and diplomatic and they may have a good nose for politics. Sharp instincts and excellent analytical ability make them good at research or investigation. Their penetrating mind permits them to give depth to their endeavors and helps them institute reform.

The Pluto-MC/IC inconjunct indicates a strong tendency to oppose established authority. These natives want to change the world. Their concern for the underdog makes them want to challenge the power of authority figures. If they could, they would force the world to reconsider the past and revise accustomed beliefs. They have strong opinions, but suffer from ambivalent rebelliousness. They want to change and reform, but also want permission to assert their power. They may be forced, instead, to cooperate against their will. They may feel pressure from their parents, family members or superiors. They may be forced to deal with manipulative or controlling authorities who cannot accept change. This pattern exists until they learn to act without first seeking permission.

There may be an obsessive concern with career success and personal power. These natives want success for the power and recognition it brings. They want to be able to act effectively and make things happen. They can be jealous of other people's success and resent those who attain the authority they desire. They must eventually resolve the conflict between the need for career success and the desire for a fulfilling family life. In order to do this, they need to set priorities and then live by them. Once these natives attain power they find themselves with the challenge of learning how to delegate it, for they can become willful or tyrannical. Their inability to relinquish power and a tendency to overcontrol subordinates eventually engenders resentment and opposition. A tendency to hold onto the past and carry on vendettas ultimately undermines their position. Therefore, it is essential to learn to let things pass. Those who opt for family instead of career fulfillment may become family tyrants if they aren't careful. The tendency to dominate family members creates resentment and rebellion. They need to learn how to lighten up.

This aspect indicates a tendency to develop rigid or dogmatic views.

These natives can be doctrinaire. They can't seem to let go of old feelings, especially resentments. They can't seem to let go of old methodology either. Fear of uncertainty seems to make them unspontaneous and stilted. Inflexible views and rigid agendas preclude adjustment and inhibit career success. Some natives have to confront dogmatic authorities who refuse to reconsider rigid beliefs. They eventually learn to approach people with tact and diplomacy in order to effect change.

This inconjunct indicates a persistence that can make these natives excellent investigators or researchers. An interest in motivation might assist them in careers in acting, sales or in psychology. This aspect also might be used by systems analysts, politicians or X-ray technicians.

PART THREE
Jimmy Carter's
Chart

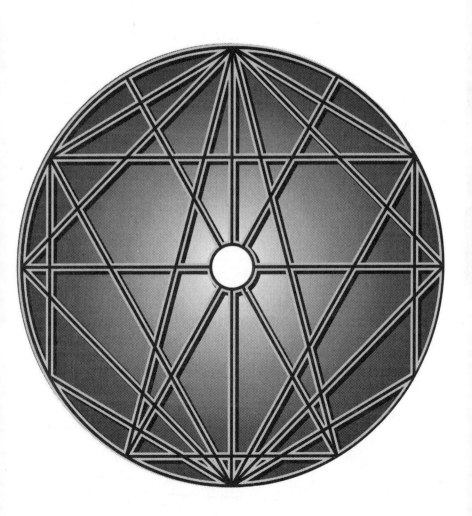

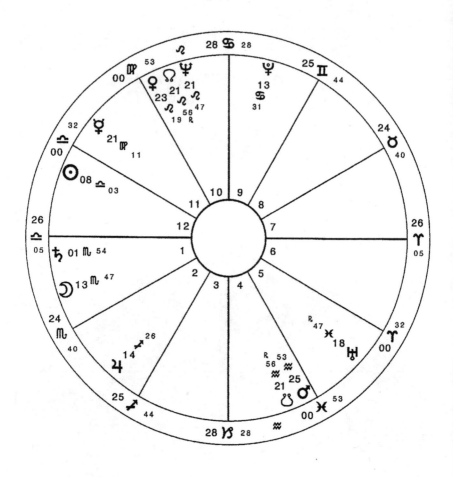

Jimmy Carter

Oct 1 1924	7:00 AM CST
Plains	Georgia
32N02	84W24
Oct 1 1924	13:00:00 GMT

Tropical   Placidus   True Node

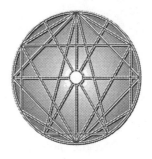

Jimmy Carter's Chart

Introduction

THIS SECTION PRESENTS AN IN DEPTH CHART ANALYSIS to illustrate the practical application of the material in the preceding sections. Jimmy Carter's chart was chosen because it provides an outstanding example of inconjuncts in action. As we analyze Carter's chart, we can recall the difficulties that arose in his personal life and in his presidency. We may, perhaps, better appreciate the man for his successes, failures and attempts to cope with crises. Jimmy Carter is exemplary in his ability to turn difficult aspects to positive use and meet challenges with persistence and faith. I feel it is, therefore, fitting that we take the time to try to understand him and allow ourselves to be influenced by his example of personal excellence.

Major Events

Jimmy Carter was born James Earl Carter Jr. on October 1, 1924, at 7:00 AM, CST, in Plains, Georgia, a small rural village. The first of four children, he grew up with the privileges and burdens of the eldest son of a farmer-entrepreneur. Farm life was difficult, requiring hard work and long hours. Jimmy Carter was a serious boy, an obedient son, hard working, and an excellent student. Early in life, he decided upon a career in the navy, set his goals upon entering Annapolis and worked diligently toward that end. The opportunity finally came in the summer of 1943, and he made the most of it, graduating in 1946 in the top ten percent of his class. During this time, he met Rosalynn Smith, a friend of his sister Ruth, and married her on July 7, 1946. The couple looked upon Jimmy's naval career with excitement, and saw it as an opportunity to expand their horizons and escape from the humdrum life of a rural village. Carter soon volunteered to serve in the Submarine Service because it was the most dangerous, elite and, therefore, the most challenging. It also offered the possibility for the swiftest advancement in responsibility and grade. The difficult work was personally challenging – Carter excelled. Duties kept him separated from Rosalynn, and she had to handle family affairs single-handedly. The Carters managed, however, to have three sons during this period.

In January 1951, Carter went to see Admiral Rickover about the possibility of serving under him in the new Atomic Submarine fleet. He was accepted, and toiled under Rickover, who was a critical and severe taskmaster. Carter soon began to appreciate the Admiral's thoroughness and discipline, and came to regard him with respect and admiration. He spent many long days under Rickover, becoming an expert in Nuclear Engineering, and was on his way to a successful career in the military, when disaster struck. Carter's father died in July 1953 and left the family finances in a shambles. After much agonizing, Carter decided to sacrifice his own promising career, resign his commission, and return to Plains to rescue the family business from bankruptcy and the family name from humiliation. He settled his wife and three children in a public housing project and took over the family business, having no finances and a great deal of naivete about farming as a business. In typical Jimmy Carter fashion, he made himself, through sheer perseverance, into an expert and excelled in both the farming and promotional ends of the agricultural business. He became so successful that he was sought after as a board member of various civic, charitable and religious organizations. He pursued these responsibilities like he did everything else, with earnestness, hard work and zeal. His civic involvements soon led to an interest in running for state office. He started small, bucking the local corrupt political establishment all along the way, and eventually got himself elected to Governor of Georgia in 1970. He ran for President in 1976 and ascended to the highest office in the land in 1977.*

*Information about Carter's life from: James Wooten, *Dasher – The Roots and the Rising of Jimmy Carter,* Summit books, 1978.

Interpreting the Inconjuncts

The most striking thing about Jimmy Carter is his willpower, his ability to apply himself, work hard and devote himself to a goal. His absolute stubbornness, perseverance and unwillingness to yield in the face of difficulties and obstacles would seem more characteristic of a fixed sign that a double Libra. Many people would, of course, point to his Scorpio Moon and Saturn rising in Scorpio as the prominent influences toward this end. Pluto square the Sun and Mars in a fixed sign would also be seen as reinforcing these qualities. There are, however, additional important influences: the Sun inconjunct Saturn and the Moon, and the Mars inconjuncts with Mercury, Uranus and the Midheaven.

Taken by itself, the solar inconjunct might indicate a strong need to win acceptance for oneself or one's projects. The Saturn-Sun inconjunct would give the ability to shoulder burdens, make sacrifices and persevere. This means that once Carter makes up his mind to follow a course, and adopts it as his purpose, he becomes determined and persevering, willing to accept hardships and make sacrifices. He sets his eye on his long-term goal and works toward it realistically and patiently. He will not be put off or discouraged. The solar-lunar inconjunct reinforces these concerns because it becomes a matter of personal pride not to give up or be denied. It means that he would probably find defeat humiliating and so he defiantly sticks to his purposes. Carter, thus, makes the best use of this particular inconjunct: adopting a purpose and working hard to realize the personal goals one sets. In a lesser man, this might not always be true, for the Sun-Saturn inconjunct might easily lead one to give up one's direction when confronted by obstacles and delays. It might also indicate a tendency to use burdens or responsibilities as excuses for giving up one's goals. This did, in fact, happen when Carter's father died. He had to sacrifice his own aspirations in support and acceptance of family burdens and responsibilities. The Sun-Moon inconjunct might, similarly, force one to forego one's purposes under the pressure of social disapproval. Jimmy Carter, as a man of character and inner strength turns these tendencies around, so that they serve rather than defeat him. Self-approval overcomes the pressure of social disapproval, and self-acceptance permits him to persevere until he succeeds. Carter had to give up a promising military career in order to fulfill his family responsibilities, but he eventually turned this defeat around, entered politics and became President of the United States.

Carter also turns his Mars inconjuncts to good use, for in a lesser person these aspects might lead to impatience, inconsistency, unreliability or lack of activity. The Mars-Uranus inconjunct might be a particular source of trouble, for it can indicate either impulsiveness and violence or a bland inability to assert oneself. Carter seems to suffer from none of these problems. Instead, the rage and passion of the Mars-Uranus inconjunct seems to be sublimated into a work ethic and a drive for excellence. The need to prove oneself, indicated by the Mars inconjuncts, probably makes him both competitive and success/achievement oriented. Carter is a doer, and once he decides upon what he wants to achieve, he throws himself into the task wholeheartedly, with his whole store of aggression, which is sizeable, until success is his.

Looking at the psychodynamics of the inconjuncts tempts one to speculate about the possible roots of these remarkable qualities. I will attempt this, as an exercise, but with a disclaimer: This is merely a speculative exercise, based upon theoretical considerations. Without feedback and mutual interaction that's all it can be – a speculative exercise.

According to biographer James Wooten in *Dasher – The Roots And The Rising of Jimmy Carter*, Carter was the apple of his parents' eyes, but his second sister, Ruth, eventually supplanted him, especially in relation to their father. Around the time that Ruth was born, Earl Carter practically forced his son Jimmy to begin hard work – by making him start his own little peanut business. Five year old Jimmy began to pick and strip peanuts, early in the morning, boil them, package them and take them to town on his little wagon, where he would sell them to the locals. He, at first, had to endure much kidding from the grown-ups, but eventually gained their acceptance, sold his peanuts and came home with money in his pockets. This pleased his father greatly. Little Jimmy would deposit his money in his bureau drawer, and then return the next day to repeat the process of harvesting, processing and selling peanuts. This may be one of the roots of his propensity for hard work: little Jimmy becoming a big boy to please Father and win his acceptance (Sun inconjunct Saturn). It is possible that in the mind of a five-year-old child, Father becoming severe and demanding at the same time little sister is born might be interpreted as rejection by Father. But … Father, being basically good and fair, could be won over. Hard work and personal responsibility, the virtues Father admired, would become the key to his acceptance and respect. The rage that Jimmy might have felt at the birth of his sibling usurper (Uranus in the fifth house inconjunct Mars in the fourth – the fifth house being the second sibling) would have been sublimated into hard work to please and prove himself to Father (Mars inconjunct the Mid-heaven). But, he would have gained this at a cost. The ability to take violent action would be given up in order to win the acknowledgment from authority figures. This would prove to be a problem later on when it came time to deal with Khomeini, an authority figure if there ever was one.

Carter is known to be highly competitive. He fights hard to win and hates to come in second. The best is the only thing good enough for Jimmy Carter. Achievement is a key aim. He toils for his success and he earns everything he gets. This is another manifestation of Mars inconjunct the Midheaven. He works hard to further of his career and his place in the world. He works hard for the acknowledgment of authority figures, probably starting first with his father and then with Admiral Rickover. Carter is, most especially, intellectually competitive (Mars inconjunct Mercury). He always was an academic achiever and always ranked at or near the top of his class. He is, in many ways, self-made, especially intellectually, and has more than once made himself expert in fields as diverse as nuclear physics and agriculture. He has a tremendous capacity to read and devour extraordinary amounts of information. However, brilliant as he is, he still has difficulty conveying his ideas and expressing himself verbally. His twangy singsong voice, tendency to bunch phrases together, accentuate the wrong words and trail off at the end of a sentence create difficulties in public speaking. Carter, aware and upset over this deficiency, took professional voice lessons, but to no avail. These difficulties are the probable manifestations of a Mercury inconjunct, and Carter has three such aspects: Mercury inconjunct the Ascendant/Descendant axis; Mercury inconjunct the Venus-Neptune conjunction; Mercury inconjunct Mars. One might suppose that with Libra rising and Venus conjunct Neptune in the Midheaven sextile the Ascendant, Carter would express himself better. But, the Mercury inconjuncts, reinforced by Saturn rising, overcome the advantages of a Libra Ascendant and a prominent Venus.

The Mercury inconjuncts are made more interesting here by the combination of planets and angles involved. The Mercury-ASC/DSC inconjunct often guarantees some Mercury-related anomaly as a personal characteristic. Typical of such anomalies are unique speech patterns, speech defects, an emphasis upon intellectualism, intellectual defensiveness, redundancy, a need to win support for one's views or a tendency to alter one's expression in order to preclude antagonism. The Mercury-Venus contradicts the Mercury-Mars aspect because the former wants to win people over while the latter wants to verbally attack others or assert the validity of unpopular ideas. This creates a double bind, for how can one attack others and still win them over? The solution may come from the Mercury/Neptune inconjunct: speak vaguely, in symbols, be ambivalent, make things appear less forceful than they really are (hence a singsong voice saying important and powerful things). One might again speculate upon the psychodynamic roots of this behavior and suppose that it permitted a good, respectful, obedient son the possibility of asserting himself or his views against conservative parental authority. One further thing about this aspect: once Jimmy Carter gives his word or makes a commitment he keeps it. "You can consider it done," he will say, and it is true. Once he makes a clear commitment he considers it an obligation to be fulfilled (Mercury-Neptune inconjunct).

Carter is known for, among other things, being extremely tight with his money. He is, in fact, considered by many to be a tightwad. This might, at first, seem strange given his second house Sagittarian Jupiter and his Venus-Neptune conjunction in Leo in the tenth house. One might, of course, again point to Saturn rising as the prominent influence in this direction, but there is much more to it than that. For one thing, the second house Jupiter is exactly inconjunct his ninth house Pluto (the ruler of his second house). This means that he can be obsessed with holding onto what he owns. Pluto inconjuncts tend to make one resist change, avoid uncertainty and demand security. They also tend to make one stick to inflexible plans and keep to rigid agendas. Planning becomes all important and uncertainty a thing to be avoided. It may be that control is the chief virtue here, so that it becomes essential not to lose control over one's assets. The complication in this is the prominent Moon-Jupiter inconjunct. This means that one might be tempted to purchase approval through financial generosity. Apparently, this describes Carter's mother more than it describes him. Miz Lillian was always generous with indigent neighbors and sought to help them whenever she could. She was said to be a human CARE package and she did, in fact, join the Peace Corps when she was sixty-seven years old. Jupiter-Moon inconjuncts might, in general, indicate fears of abandonment, and betrayal, and a need, perhaps, to win approval through generosity or helpfulness. It may, perhaps, suggest amassing of finances or resources as a strategy for winning approval or as a buffer against feelings of abandonment or betrayal. Venus inconjunct the Midheaven might reinforce this reluctance to part with money. Venus inconjuncts, in general, indicate a tendency to feel unworthy and/ or intrinsically unlovable. It tends to make one feel a need to earn love, affection or appreciation. When Venus is inconjunct the MC/IC axis, it may indicate a tendency to deny oneself satisfaction in the attempt to win over authority figures. And, there is often a great deal of resentment in the feeling of having to forego one's own happiness just to satisfy authorities (usually parental). It might sometimes cause the native to accumulate money or to be reluctant to part with it, if it becomes a compensation for lost satisfaction. If the feeling of having to forego comfort and happiness is intermingled with feelings of resentment at having to sacrifice one's pleasure, this might cause one to resist sharing or wasting money because money represents hard work, sacrifice and emotional investment. Some of these considerations might have validity, given Carter's childhood background of a stern father who considered industry a prime virtue.

Carter's Moon-Jupiter inconjunct manifested in striking ways during the term of his presidency. Lunar inconjuncts, in general, create issues around loyalty/betrayal, approval/disapproval and shame/embarrassment. The Moon here as ruler of the tenth house reinforces its public quality, so that Carter would feel publicly betrayed and/or embarrassed. By what? By the other end of the lunar inconjunct: Jupiter inconjunct issues. These include excessiveness, exaggeration, bad judgments, opinions and beliefs, waste and unfulfilled expectations. And, since Jupiter rules his third house (siblings) and is in his second house (money), it involves his brother Billy and money issues. We might remember how often Carter was embarrassed over his brother's opinions and public statements, his financial dealings with Libya (Jupiter in the second house inconjunct Pluto in the ninth house — Billy was going to be a public relations man for a foreign dictator), and his excess (drinking problem). In all of this, Jimmy had to control his feelings publicly (lunar inconjunct) and maintain his calmness and equanimity, even though he must have felt betrayed (lunar inconjunct).

We have mentioned some of the Mercury inconjunct manifestations: Carter's desire to prove himself through intellectual challenge and an inability to speak well in public. Carter does, however, have a wonderful facility for speaking around an issue, creating a vaguely satisfying impression (Mercury inconjunct Venus and Neptune). He seems to be able to take any situation that comes up and explain it in a way that allays fears and puts people at ease. The Venus-Neptune inconjunct Mercury gives him the ability to sell his ideas or explanations, even if he doesn't express them well verbally. In fact, his speech problems may actually work in his favor because they lend an air of vulnerability which creates sympathy. Whatever it actually does, it seems to get people to place their trust in him.

The Venus-Neptune inconjunct the MC/IC did, however, create some difficult problems during his administration. For one thing, Venus-

Neptune inconjunct the MC/IC, reinforced by Jupiter inconjunct the Moon and Jupiter inconjunct Pluto, eventually came to fruition as the tremendous inflation which plagued the latter years of his term. In fact, inflation was one of the prime causes, if not the prime cause, of his eventual public disfavor (Jupiter-Moon inconjunct and Venus-Neptune-Midheaven inconjunct) and probably cost him the 1980 election.

We have already touched upon some of the Mars inconjunct manifestations: Carter's ability to sublimate his anger, intensify his efforts and apply himself intellectually. We mentioned also that it might be difficult for Carter to attack or be aggressive with authority figures, and suggested that this might have been part of his problem in dealing with Khomeini, a Saturnian authority figure, if there ever was one. During the height of the hostage crisis, Carter showed the utmost restraint, to no avail, for Khomeini merely interpreted his lack of strong action as weakness. This is typical of Mars inconjunct the MC: one feels unable to assert oneself in the face of authority. One just isn't used to it. Frustration and resentment builds up until one finally takes strong action. But, such action is often fruitless because of the predisposition to impotence in the face of authority. The day finally came (4/24/80) when Carter could take it no longer. He, apparently, felt compelled, through a combination of personal frustration and political pressure, to take strong measures. He ordered the helicopter rescue attempt and failed miserably, humiliatingly. At the time, the transiting Mars was approaching 28 Leo, forming an inconjunct to his Midheaven.

Carter did, however, make good use of both his Mars inconjunct MC and his Venus-Neptune inconjunct MC during his term of office. He fulfilled the Libra function of mediation and got Egypt and Israel to sign the historic peace treaty on March 26, 1979. It was only Jimmy Carter's perseverance that kept the negotiations going, and the treaty is a testimony to his spiritual power. Interestingly enough, the treaty was signed when the transiting Mars was at 21 Pisces 13 (1/2 degree from an inconjunct to his natal Neptune and exactly opposite his natal Mercury) and the transiting Venus was at 27 Aquarius 13 (inconjunct his MC). Carter, thus, made optimal use of his natal Mars-MC and Venus-MC aspects: Being a peacemaker. Of course, in another chart, the Mars-MC inconjunct might indicate the use of force to change society. So, the manifestation depends upon the spirit of the native.

President Carter presents a good example of the difficulties and potential pitfalls of the inconjunct. His public career shows how these aspects may be turned to constructive use. Carter reveals himself as a highly productive, spiritual individual, with a strong will and desire for the good.

His strength of character and willingness to make sacrifices permits him to be a positive force in this troubled world and allows him to succeed at tasks lesser men would find insurmountable.

About the Author

Alan Epstein was born in Brooklyn, New York on January 24, 1939. He attended CCNY, studying physics and engineering, graduating in 1961. He worked for the U.S. Army as a project engineer (6th house Sun opposite Pluto, 8th house Moon opposite Neptune) and project manager, for 25 years, developing military weapons systems, and representing the U.S. Army at international forums.

In 1969, Alan discovered the teachings of Krishnamurti, which changed his life. This renewed his focus on self-observation and self-searching, to uncover the hidden influences that govern his and other people's lives. In the following years meditation, psychotherapy, and astrology became important tools for self-discovery and understanding. He began studying astrology with Eleanor Bach in 1974, and studied a number of psychological systems, including the teachings of Freud, Jung, Assagioli, Wilhelm Reich, and Akhter Ahsen. Reich and Ahsen, along with Krishnamurti and Astrology, eventually became key influences in his philosophy of life. NLP and the teachings of Lester Levenson became additional influences in recent years.

The first incarnation of this book was published in 1984 by Samuel Weiser, Inc. Since that time, Alan has lectured on the Inconjunct and on other astrological topics for local, as well as national astrological organizations. He was the keynote speaker at the 1987 NORWAC conference, has lectured for the American Federation of Astrologers, the Fraternity for Canadian Astrologers in their Toronto and Montreal conferences, and the National Council for Geocosmic Research in New York and San Francisco. He was the founder and president (1983-1986) of the Association of Astrology and Psychology (AAP), in New York City, which conducted ambitious programs and conferences to bring together the two disciplines. Since that time, perhaps as a result of some small influence by AAP, astrologers have pursued degrees in psychology and psychotherapists have become interested in astrology.

Alan now lives in Reno, Nevada where he writes, lectures on astrology and organizes conferences. He has been focusing on understanding the aspects, and future publications will address the other astrological aspects from both a psychological and spiritual perspective. He spends his free time hiking around Lake Tahoe and the Sierras, listening to classical music, and wondering what life is all about. The results of these speculations will, no doubt, appear in future writings.

For more information on
UNDERSTANDING ASPECTS: The Inconjunct
by Alan Epstein
and/ or to receive a free copy of
the TRINES Newsletter call:
1-800-500-8480

or write to:

TRINES PUBLISHING

P.O. Box 20548
Reno, Nevada 89515-0548
USA

Alan Epstein is available for talks, lectures, workshops and seminars in your area. If you want to be on his mailing list please call or write at the above phone number and address.

Alan Epstein audio tapes are available.